The
Garland Library
of
War and Peace

The
Garland Library
of
War and Peace

Under the General Editorship of
Blanche Wiesen Cook, *John Jay College, C.U.N.Y.*
Sandi E. Cooper, *Richmond College, C.U.N.Y.*
Charles Chatfield, *Wittenberg University*

Five Views on European Peace

Reorganization of the European Community

by

Henri Comte de Saint-Simon

The United States of Europe

by

Victor Hugo

Considerations on the Political System Now Existing in Europe

by

Friedrich von Gentz

Europe: Its Condition and Prospects

by

Giuseppe Mazzini

Dernière Guerre et la paix définitive en Europe

by

Victor Considérant

with a new introduction
for the Garland Edition by

Sandi E. Cooper

Garland Publishing, Inc., New York & London
1972

Library of Congress Cataloging in Publication Data
Main entry under title:

Five views on European peace.

(The Garland library of war and peace)
CONTENTS: Reorganization of the European community,
by H. C. de Saint-Simon [first published 1814].--The
United States of Europe, by V. Hugo [first published
1914].--Considerations on the political system now
existing in Europe, by F. von Gentz [first published
1818]. [etc.]
    1. Peace. 2. Europe--Politics--1789-1900.
I. Series.
JX1963.F612 1972   320.9'4'028   72-4159
ISBN 0-8240-0219-9

Introduction

The years of the French Revolution and the Napoleonic conquest of Europe revealed an undeniable conjunction between international war and internal revolution, a combination which both repelled and attracted contemporary and successive generations. Represented in this volume are excerpts from five eminent Europeans who lived, wrote and worked in the shadow of that awesome reality. Though their attitudes toward war and revolution differ sharply, the observations of Saint-Simon, Gentz, Hugo, Mazzini and Considérant reflect the responses of a wide range of committed and thoughtful Europeans.

The unifying thread binding these diverse commentators is their mutual recognition that the international order of the ancien régime was destroyed. Under no conditions could the sovereign dynastic state, its monarchs and ministers, lightly engage in warfare again. The battlefield as a playground for restless royal spirits had become a seeding ground for revolution. This understanding is vividly clear in the first two selections from Saint-Simon and Gentz. The last three authors wrote with the added experience of thirty-three years of the "Metternichean" system which, of course, collapsed in the revolutions of

1848, and, at least on the international level, was not revived in the restorations of 1849. For Hugo, Mazzini and Considérant, the memories of the French Revolutionary era were dimmer than their immediate consciousness of the frustrations of oppressed nationalities, official and officious indifference to the yearnings of peoples for civil and political rights, and the newer demands for social rights linked to economic equality. These three had just witnessed the drama of the springtime of 1848 and then, the repressions of the winter of 1849. Generally committed to ideals of social justice and liberal nationalism, though to different means for their attainment, these three writers and activists also saw the urgent necessity of a union of peoples based on, but transcending, lines of nationality. Their vision, at least in the wake of 1848-49, was designed to uplift the depressed and defeated of the revolutions that failed. Mazzini, of course, was himself one of those deeply involved in the collapse of the dreams of 1848. Their humanism and humanitarianism lifted nationalism to its highest theoretical level and made it the basis of internationalism.

Saint-Simon prepared his essay which his pupil Augustin Thierry revised for publication in October, 1814 with the faint hope that the gentlemen gathered in Vienna to liquidate the Napoleonic legacy, might pay some attention to a set of dramatically new principles regarding the creation and maintenance of peace. Fortunately he was too much a realist to

INTRODUCTION

delude himself into thinking they would really listen but he issued The Reorganization of the European Community anyway for the benefit of future generations.

Scholars have long admired Saint-Simon for his apparent prescience about the requirements and contours of the coming age of industrialization, if not for his generally chaotic style of writing. In recent years, his reputation has spread beyond a narrow circle, mainly French, and he has become an important addition to that very creative group of social theorists which flourished in the early nineteenth century.[1]

For Saint-Simon, the old system of balance of power and alliances was antiquated as a means for preserving peace. He surveyed the forms which preserved peace in previous epochs to determine what universal principles might be adduced and adopted by succeeding ages. He is careful to draw the line between the specific historic conditions in which any given form worked and the underlying principles of its operation. Next, contemporary forces are analyzed. Old means of ordering societies no longer functioned but new ones had not yet developed. Hints, shoots and promises of new forms and forces which would shape civilization in the future

[1]Students interested in good, brief introductions to his ideas are referred to Frank E. Manuel, The Prophets of Paris: Turgot, Condorcet, Saint-Simon, Fourier, Comte (Harper Torchbooks, 1965) and Henri de Saint-Simon, Social Organization. The Science of Man and other writings, ed. by Felix Markham (Harper Torchbooks, 1964).

7

INTRODUCTION

abounded. Saint-Simon expected the new era would be managed by the élites of science, the professions and businessmen replacing the role and manners of the aristocratic, privileged society. Such a coming age required new institutions of all sorts, including a fresh and creative approach to the management of international affairs.

Thus, from his discussion of past, present and future, from his insistence on intelligent planning by experts, from his view that political orders must be responsive to changes in social orders, Saint-Simon argued for a new form of interstate relations capable of preserving peace and freed from royal-aristocratic control. His plan derived from, but also rejected an older peace project of the previous century devised by the Abbé de Saint-Pierre. This scheme for international government had also been composed in the wake of approximately twenty-five years of European war, as the heads of state gathered to negotiate the peace of the early eighteenth century.[2] What Saint-Simon rejected in the Abbé's plan was its apparent rigidity that did not take into account the possibility of change within states. The project seemed to ratify permanently the status quo of the day when sovereigns would subscribe to it. The Abbé certainly ought not be penalized for dealing with eighteenth and not nineteenth century realities. Saint-Simon, however, was rightly concerned about perpetuating the forms

[2] *The project of the Abbé de Saint-Pierre will appear in* Peace Projects of the Eighteenth Century *in this series.*

8

of one age into the dynamic new age to come. He knew that any system which obstructed new forces was an invitation to a renewal of war and revolution. In many ways, what Saint-Simon warned against was precisely what the Congress system, created at Vienna, attempted to establish — and maintained at least until 1848. From one point of view, the Congress system was a fulfilment of Saint-Pierre's recommendations but adopted one century too late.

Saint-Simon's project for a total reorganization of the European state system linked international peace with social justice and economic expansion. This deserves recognition. The connection of peace in the international order with satisfaction of needs in the social order was a relationship which not even most pacifists and peace advocates subsequently accepted.

To the modern ear, the mechanics and specific institutional recommendations he made for the new order among European states might sound awkward or embarrassing but a second look brings the shock of recognition. A good many of the post-World War II agencies quartered in Brussels and Geneva bear striking resemblance to the councils of experts proposed in 1814 in this essay. Saint-Simon discarded as functionless the traditional diplomatic machinery and contacts between ministers and heads of states. In place, he proposed an international parliament modeled on the "best" principles then available for successful governments — the constitutions of England and France. Such a body was far more appro-

priate to post-revolutionary and pre-industrial Europe. Qualifications for participation in the houses of this parliament, qualifications for voting, the division of authority in the parliament were all discussed again with an eye to the English and French experiences.

From the establishing of international governing institutions, there would emanate slowly over time the binding force of international patriotism. Hence would develop a universalistic spirit commanding allegiance akin to that once exercised by the Church in earlier centuries. Neither the notion of a balance of power nor a confederation of sovereigns could produce the type of popular fidelity which Saint-Simon recognized as a prerequisite for successful internationalism.

To begin, he recommended the formation of a single state by an alliance of the French and English. Included in the selection here are a variety of reasons which Saint-Simon offered to demonstrate why each would benefit from such a radical departure from history. This association would be the core and would create the basic institutions. He is vague about how other states would join, though in the section on Germany, there is a clear implication that the Anglo-French axis would have to help progressive German forces wage a "limited" revolution before that people could be added.

It was an all important feature of Saint-Simon's project that the national regimes of the constituent states be ordered on constitutional lines similar to the international government. Furthermore, the European reorganization he had in mind was one which worked for the elimination of feudal vestiges. Thus, while Saint-Simon offered his program in an effort to create an international system that would obviate the need for revolution, the inauguration of his system itself required certain radical changes, at least in the Europe of 1814. His notion of revolution bore no resemblance to the popular, Jacobin form of 1793-94 through which he lived and which he cordially hated, by 1814. Rather, it is the revolutionary activity of the enlightened professional, entrepreneurial and scientific leadership against the non-functioning remnants of privilege and caste.

While an Anglo-French axis formed the core of Saint-Simon's projected European parliament, the solid cooperation of Austria and Prussia was pronounced the sine qua non *of European peace by Friedrich von Gentz. On the Continent, von Gentz was second to Edmund Burke in his reputation as a stalwart anti-revolutionary.[3] Indeed, von Gentz himself had translated and disseminated Burke's work on the Continent. Besides denouncing revolution as breeding only anarchy and chaos, von Gentz was impatient of reform of so-called social abuses and*

---

[3] *Students might be interested in his anti-revolutionary essay against France available in English in Stefan Possony, ed.,* Three Revolutions *(Chicago: Henry Regnery & Co.) Gentz' attack on the French Revolution was originally made available to Americans by John Adams.*

11

detested such men as the Prussian Baron von Stein for his efforts. As secretary to Clemens von Metternich, von Gentz was intimate with the core of policy making at the Congress of Vienna and after.

Why is von Gentz included here? Certainly, he is no pacifist and was quite comfortable justifying the use of force in the suppression of revolution or unrest. Nonetheless, by 1815, he was well aware of the dangers implicit in a return to the old state system which permitted too capricious, too independent judgments on the part of sovereigns on the question of war. In the post-Napoleonic age, the old system of power blocs was insufficient. What was necessary for a concerted agreement among decision makers to resolve their differences by discussion — a system of Congresses in which heads of state would meet. Hence, Gentz and Metternich must be added to the ranks of "internationalists" if not pacifists. For whatever motives, theirs was a vision of "collective security."

Gentz' opening remarks describe the new system devised by The Congress of Vienna. To overcome the weakness inherent in the alliance system and the balance of power as the machinery for keeping peace, there has been added the "principle of general union, uniting all states collectively with a federative bond, under the guidance of the five principal Powers . . . ." Within the "grand political family" thus formed in Europe, the greater Powers exercised preponderant authority in decision making which

INTRODUCTION

Gentz believed was justified and realistic. The members of the union would meet periodically, as indeed they did in 1818 at Aix-la-Chapelle, 1820-21 at Troppau and Laibach, and in 1822 at Verona. In 1820, when revolutions broke forth in Naples and Spain, the Austrians and French exercised their big-power duties as members of the union and sent troops to intervene and suppress the risings.

As is well known and needs little discussion here, the British soon decided to remove themselves form full cooperation with the Congress system. British support of the Monroe Doctrine, essentially tacit support of Latin American independence from Spain, followed by British support of Greek and Belgian revolutionary aspirations essentially turned the Congress system into an organization affecting central and eastern Europe. Gentz, of course, did not foresee this contingency.

However, he was not unaware that the system might not work. His piece discussed the centripetal forces which could pull apart the system. He clearly saw that the nature of the sovereign state, particularly its desire to exercise independent postures in foreign policy making, was a historic right which a system, created during an emergency, might not transform. As the mutual fear inspired by Napoleon's return from Elba subsided, the glue cementing the system could dry up. At best, Gentz hoped it would work for a generation at least until Austria, particularly, recouped her strength. What would ensue as a set of

INTRODUCTION

international arrangements is not discussed here. Probably Gentz expected the states would resume the older alliance system and even resort to war, when it was safe enough. "Safe enough" means, of course, that the possibility of revolution during a war would not be imminent and that a generation of peace maintained by the collective arrangement of the Congress system would be sufficient to dull the impulses toward revolution.

The selection from Gentz illustrates one form of "official" thinking about the utility and maintenance of peace. It would be a mistake to view this position as simply a product of his time and place. That peace is desirable to groups representing "conservative" interests is not unique to the generation of politicians following 1814-15. For twentieth century students, there is something familiar about the notion that major state establishments composed of similar social systems ought lay aside war as a means of resolving conflict, when faced with threats to their social orders. Further, that the establishments of one state have an obligation to restore and maintain the social order of another, which entails intervention into a sister sovereignty, is not an unusual event in the post World War II world. And then, the apprehension expressed by Gentz about that "unknown" and mysterious entity in European politics, Russia, certainly rings familiar.

The brief excerpt from the master littérateur, Victor Hugo, contained in this volume reflects one of

INTRODUCTION

his great personal commitments — his interest in internationalism and peace. Originally delivered as the presidential address to the Peace Congress of Paris on August 22, 1849, it was reprinted by the American World Peace Foundation when "the lamps went out" in 1914. Hugo was elected president of the Peace Congress, which was an early example of an international gathering of peace workers and their sympathizers of mainly English, French and American background. Alexis de Tocqueville and Richard Cobden were also present. The participants were, in Hugo's words, "publicists, philosophers, ministers of Christian sects, eminent writers, numerous persons of importance in public life — the luminaries of the nations." [4] *Hugo praised the delegates and encouraged them to continue in their labors, although the general public might not be ready for their message. He had no doubt that one day their cause — world peace — would be embraced enthusiastically by civilized men and these early crusaders would be hailed as realists rather than scorned as utopians.*

Hugo's speech, besides giving currency to the phrase "The United States of Europe", is an excellent statement of the idealism of the fledgling peace movement of the mid-nineteenth century. This movement, dissolved temporarily with the Crimean War, was the first important association of peace workers across national lines. Its existence remained as in-

[4] Victor Hugo, "Discours d'ouverture, 21 août, 1849," in Douze Discours, (Paris, La Librairie Nouvelle, 1851), p. 16.

spiration for a revitalization of the movement and the cause in the later decades of the nineteenth century. During its day, however, it was most commonly charged with being a movement of utopians, if not crackpots. Most of the ideology it embraced derived from the free trade and peace position of Richard Cobden's group in England.

Hugo attempted to refute the charge of utopianism. He pointed to the history of France as a model. Four centuries before, who would have dared predict that the warring provinces — Lorraine, Picardy, Normandy, Brittany, Auvergne, Provence, Dauphiné, Burgundy — would be joined in a single political unit. That their differences would be settled in a "small box of wood — a ballot box" and in "an assembly . . . which shall be . . . the soul of all" was not foreseen. Hugo observed, further, that war in the nineteenth century was falling into disuse. In an age where nations were increasingly bound together by commercial relationships and kinships evolving from mutually accepted ideas, war was a pointless mechanism. Civilized nations marched forward in a direction which bound them closer and closer and made archaic the traditional processes of statecraft. Thus, he foresaw the day when the individual states of Europe would form a single legislative assembly, would develop the means to settle their differences in a legal system and would turn the enormous quantities of wealth presently used for military purposes into the development of resources at home and the export of civilization to Asia and Africa. Hugo's canvas depicting a landscape of Europe at peace provided an answer to the causes of revolution for once the national riches were deployed in useful projects, social misery would decline. His purpose was to broadcast the message of the peace movement and to hearten the peace workers into a further commitment to the cause.

Of the last three writers included in this volume, Hugo represents the position most opposed to war in any form, for any value or purpose. Such an absolutist position against war was not shared by Mazzini or Considérant. While these latter would have differed over questions of social justice and social responsibility, they would have agreed that war was justified under certain circumstances. Explicitly, those circumstances were the liberation of peoples from oppression.

Unlike Saint-Simon or Hugo who generally ignore the idea, Giuseppe Mazzini, famous for his years of work in the cause of Italian unification and freedom, saw no peace in Europe until the nationalities were liberated and the "map of Europe," created in 1815, was redrawn. The remaking of that map implied the continued displacement of social survivals from the past — patriciates, the Papacy, multinational imperialisms, the thirty-five separate German sovereignties, the façades of legitimacy devised by Vienna, and of course, the tragic separation of Italians. When, and only when, the right to associate in free states

17

with one's national brothers would be secured, then, in Mazzini's vision, could the true association of all nationalisms — internationalism — emerge. Mazzini never imagined that the peoples would do unto each other what kings and aristocrats had done for centuries. Perhaps if that awful possibility had dawned upon him, he would have been disabled for his lifelong struggle, the liberation and unification of Italy.

In this essay, he wrote "nationality ought only to be to humanity that which the division of labour is in a workshop — the recognized symbol of association . . . ." Each of the national groups is endowed with a particular mission in the Europe of the future; the particular mission of Italy is to lead the way. Thus could Mazzini refute the charge levelled by Continental conservatives that England was harboring a collection of revolutionaries whose presence disturbed the order of Europe. What disturbed that order, countered Mazzini, was the groundswell of recognition among peoples of their identity and their own wish for liberation. The few revolutionaries who found refuge in England were symbols, not causes.

In his brief polemic, Victor Considérant also recognized the problem of submerged national energies. While in general his work as a publicist was confined to questions of social and economic justice, he was one early socialist theorist who took an interest in foreign policy and affairs. More explicitly than Mazzini, at least in the article included here,

INTRODUCTION

Considèrant predicted the coming of one great, final war between the forces representing modern life and those of the past. The former included free constitutional regimes, industrialization, printing, steam, law and labor while the latter were relics of barbarism and war — feudalism, monarchical and aristocratic constitutions, militarism. In the main, however, Considèrant was launching an appeal to the progressive elements in France and Germany, to the bourgeoisie, to overcome their fears of social democracy and recognize the need to join with workers' groups. He begged the bourgeoisies to abandon their tacit support of feudal forces and join the side which their position and history demanded.

Given the behaviour of certain middle class elements in the repressions of 1849, Considèrant touched on a serious and difficult problem which, of course, was more fully elaborated by Karl Marx.[5] No doubt numerous modern revolutionary theorists would scorn his reformist appeal to the middle classes for aid in a revolutionary drive. Nonetheless, his was a realistic, if futile, approach for that moment. Considèrant never betrays unalloyed admiration for revolutionaries either, however. A considerable section of this pamphlet is reserved for a denunciation of various revolutionary attempts from 1830 to 1848 for their failure to act on the principle of human fraternity. It was understandable and justified that the men of 1848 failed; they deserved to be punished

[5] *See particularly* The Eighteenth Brumaire of Louis Napoleon.

19

*for their parochial egotism. "God abandoned you,"
he proclaimed. Viennese revolutionaries refused to
aid Italians gain their liberty, Frankfurt parliament-
arians ignored Italians, Danes and Slavic peoples;
Hungarians insulted Croatians; Croatians served the
Hapsburgs against other oppressed groups and the
behavior of Germans to Poles was beyond des-
cription. France failed to take up arms in her sacred
mission of helping brothers across the Rhine and
beyond the Alps. The general failure of the peoples to
associate brought on the retribution of 1849. Unlike
the revolutionaries, the reactionaries certainly indicated their capacity to associate, to share forces and to
defeat their enemies.*

*Still the optimist, Considèrant hoped that the
lessons would be learned. When the next opportunity
came, as he was sure it would, the combined
association of angry revolutionaries would be irrest-
ible. Then, the "map of Europe will make itself,
conforming to ethnographic affinities, the free expression of the will of populations; it will be the true,
natural order, a free order, a peaceful order, a stable
order." Like Mazzini, Considèrant did not envision
the possibility that nations of free men would war
upon each other.*

*Whereas Saint-Simon and Gentz, in different ways,
associated war with revolution, Mazzini and
Considèrant associated revolution with peace. Given
his socialist inclinations — influenced by the Four-
ierist model — Considèrant most explicitly desired*

20

INTRODUCTION

peace based on a social order of economic as well as legal democracy with a system of free, nationally homogeneous states. Hugo stood somewhere between or perhaps beyond them all, partly because he based his ideals too narrowly on middle class English and French social and political conditions.

Although much of the thought of these five is descriptive of nineteenth century European conditions, striking sections of their analyses remain appropriate for our time. This is so despite the vast changes both in peacetime and military technology. Who, now, does not recognize something of Saint-Simon's international councils of experts; of Gentz' community of sovereign states cooperating to prevent war and revolution and intervening when they erupt — in the name of law and order; of Hugo's notions which tie the internationalization of commerce and ideas to the coming order of peace; of Mazzini's and Considèrant's appeal for a just revolution against oppression as the last, necessary step before the beginning of a stable peace? The ideas put forth by these five were seminal sources for the last century and a half of soldiers in the cause of peace and may still be.

Sandi E. Cooper
Division of Social Sciences
Richmond College (C.U.N.Y.)

21

Reorganization of the European Community

by
Henri Comte de Saint-Simon

and
Augustin Thierry

translated by

Felix M. H. Markham

[O.C., vol. 15, pp. 153–248.]

THE REORGANIZATION OF THE EUROPEAN COMMUNITY

OR THE NECESSITY AND THE MEANS OF UNITING THE PEOPLES OF EUROPE IN A SINGLE BODY POLITIC WHILE PRESERVING FOR EACH THEIR NATIONAL INDEPENDENCE

BY

THE COMTE DE ST. SIMON
AND A. THIERRY, HIS PUPIL

Oct. 1814

PREFACE

THIS work has been hurried into print because of present circumstances; it should have appeared later, and in a more developed form. No doubt I have done myself harm in publishing it prematurely; but the author who writes in order to promote useful results must realize that his own interests count for little.

If this essay is well received by the public, a second edition will expand those points which I have not had time to develop in this first one.

It should be borne in mind that throughout this work the church will be considered only in its political relation to the varying conditions in Europe, and that the Christian religion will be regarded only as a belief which is the basis of these relations and modifies them as it gradually changes.

The progress of the human mind, the revolutions which occur in the development of knowledge, give each century its special character.

The sixteenth century was rich in theologians; or rather the predominant interest in this century was such that nearly all writers dealt with theological questions.

In the seventeenth century the arts flourished, and the masterpieces of modern literature were born.

The writers of the last century were philosophers. They opened men's eyes to the fact that the most important social institutions were founded on prejudice and superstition, and they caused the downfall

28

of these superstitions and the powers which were built on them. This was the century of revolutions and of criticism.

What will be the character of our own century? Till now, it has none. Will it simply continue on the lines laid down by the preceding century? Will our writers be nothing but echoes of the last of these philosophers? I do not think so. The progress of the human spirit, the need for universal institutions which the upheavals of Europe make so desperately urgent—all this tells me that the examination of the great political questions will be the aim of the intellectual enquiries of our times.

The philosophy of the last century was revolutionary; that of the nineteenth century must be constructive. Lack of institutions leads to the destruction of all society; outworn institutions prolong the ignorance and the prejudices of the times which produced them. Shall we be forced to choose between barbarism and stupidity? Writers of the nineteenth century, you alone can avert this frightful dilemma!

The social order has been overturned because it no longer corresponded with the level of enlightenment; it is for you to create a better order. The body politic has been dissolved; it is for you to reconstitute it. Such a task is difficult, no doubt, but it is not beyond your powers; you govern opinion, and opinion governs the world. Sustained by the hope of performing a useful service, I dare to attempt the task of a pioneer; and in this first essay I shall try to review the conditions of Europe and the means of reorganizing it. A ruler who claims to be great must foster the arts and sciences. This axiom, repeated so many times, expresses vaguely a truth which has not yet been fully grasped. The only kings who have exercised a powerful influence on the world have been those who, yielding to the movement of their age, have followed the lines marked out for them by the writings of their contemporaries. There is no need for me to give reasons for this; it is obvious. Charles V and Henry VIII were theologians and fostered theology, and certainly their reigns were more successful than that of the amorous and witty Francis I. Louis XIV outshone the beings of his age, and Louis XIV, throughout Europe, made himself the patron of literature and of those who pursued it. The eighteenth century produced only two illustrious names among its sovereigns, Catherine and Frederick the Great; and these were the friends of philosophers and the supporters of philosophy. Which kings will support with their patronage the labours of the writers of our century?

F

If but two princes, marked out by the enlightenment of their peoples to be the protectors of everything noble and good, deigned to recollect that by promoting the advancement of the human mind a king enhances his own greatness, how quickly would this re-organization of Europe be achieved—the goal of all our efforts, the end of all our labours!

TO THE PARLIAMENTS OF
FRANCE AND ENGLAND

My Lords,

Until the end of the fifteenth century, all the nations of Europe formed a single body politic, at peace within,[1] but armed against the enemies of its constitution and its independence.

The Roman Catholic religion, acknowledged from one end of Europe to the other, was the passive link of European society; the Catholic Church was the active link. Spread everywhere, and everywhere independent, recruited from every country, but possessing its own government and laws, it was the centre from which sprang the will inspiring this great social body and the impulse of its activity.

The government of the church was, like that of all the European peoples, an aristocratic hierarchy. A territory independent of any temporal domination, too large to be easily conquered, too small to enable its rulers to be conquerors, was the seat of the leaders of the church. By their power, which was exalted by opinion above the power of kings, they curbed national ambitions; by their policy they maintained a balance in Europe—a balance which was desirable in those times, though it has become pernicious when it has passed into the hands of a nation. Thus the Court of Rome ruled over the other courts, in the same way that these courts ruled over their peoples, and Europe was a vast aristocracy, divided into smaller aristocracies, all dependent on Rome, subject to its influence, judgments, and decrees.

Any institution founded on a belief ought not to outlive this belief. Luther, by undermining this traditional respect which gave the church its power, disorganized Europe. Half the European peoples emancipated themselves from the bonds of the Papacy—that is to say, they broke the one political link which bound them to the great community. The Treaty of Westphalia established a new order by a

[1] When I say 'at peace,' I mean to say, by comparison with what has happened since and is happening to-day.

political device called the balance of power. Europe was divided into two confederations which were artificially kept in equilibrium, thus giving rise to war and legalizing it; for two leagues of equal power are necessarily rivals, and rivalry cannot persist without war.

Thenceforth each power concentrated on increasing its military strength. Instead of puny handfuls of soldiers levied for the occasion and soon discharged, everywhere appeared formidable armies on a permanent footing, nearly always actively employed, for since the Treaty of Westphalia war has been the normal condition of Europe.

It is through this anarchy, which has been called and is still called the basis of international politics, that England rose to greatness. More skilful than the continental peoples she saw exactly what the balance of power meant, and by a double manœuvre realized how to turn it to her own profit and to the disadvantage of others. Separated from the continent by the sea, she ceased to have anything in common with the inhabitants of the continent, by creating her own national religion and a form of government different from the governments of Europe. Her constitution was based, no longer on prescription and custom, but on principles valid for all times and all places, on the proper basis for every constitution—the liberty and happiness of the people. Strengthened internally by a strong and healthy organization England directed her energies abroad to achieve great results. The aim of her foreign policy was universal dominion. She promoted her own sea-power, commerce, and industry, while hindering those of other countries. If arbitrary governments weighed on Europe, England supported them and reserved for herself liberty and its blessings. Her gold, her military power, her policy—all were directed towards maintaining this false balance, which, by causing the mutual destruction of the continental powers, left England free to do what she liked with impunity.

From this two-edged political system has grown the colossus of English power, which threatens to invade the whole world. By this means, England, free and happy internally, hard and despotic in her foreign policy, makes the whole of Europe her plaything, throwing it into turmoil at her pleasure. Such a state of affairs is too monstrous to continue. It is to the interest of Europe to free herself from a galling tyranny; it is to the interest of England to act before an armed Europe liberates herself by force.

Let there be no deception: these are not evils which can be healed by secret negotiations, by minor cabinet manœuvres. There will be no repose or happiness for Europe, as long as there is no political link to attach England again to the continent from which she has been separated.

Formerly Europe consisted of a federal community united by common institutions, subject to a common government which was in the same relation to the different peoples as national governments are to individuals; a similar organization is the only one which can effect a complete cure. Of course, I do not suggest that this outworn institution which still encumbers Europe with its useless remains should be raised from the dust—the nineteenth century is too remote from the thirteenth century.

A constitution, strong in itself, based on principles derived from the nature of things and independent of beliefs which lose their force, and of ephemeral opinions—that is what Europe needs, and what I now put forward.

Just as revolutions in States, when they come about through the progress of enlightenment, bring a better order, so the political crisis which has dissolved the European body politic was, at the same time, paving the way for a better organization. This reorganization cannot be achieved suddenly, at one stroke; for outworn institutions only gradually collapse, and better ones are only gradually built; they rise and fall slowly and insensibly.

The English people, more of a sea-faring people than the other European peoples because more insular, and therefore freer from prejudices and hereditary customs, took the first step, by replacing the feudal government by a form of government hitherto unknown. The crumbling remains of the old European organization persisted throughout the continent: governments maintained their original form, although slightly modified in some areas; the power of the church, repudiated in the North, remained in the South nothing but an instrument of subjection for the people and of despotism for the rulers. However, the human mind did not remain inactive: enlightenment spread and completed everywhere the ruin of ancient institutions. Abuses were corrected, errors destroyed, but nothing new was put in their place. The defect lay in the fact that the reforming spirit needed the backing of a political force, and, as this force lay in England alone, it was unable to struggle against the forces of the whole continent which acted as the bastion of all that remained of arbitrary rule and papal authority.

Now that France is in a position to join England in the support of liberal principles, it only remains to unite and direct these forces, and Europe will be reorganized.

This union is possible, because France is now free like England; the union is necessary, because it alone can ensure the peace of the two countries and save them from the evils which threaten them; the union can change the state of Europe, because England and France together are stronger than the rest of Europe.

The writer can only show what is to be done; the execution of it is for those who have power.

My lords, you alone can hasten this revolution of Europe, which began centuries ago, and will come about by the force of events, but only with a slowness which would be disastrous.

It is not only in the interest of your own reputations, but in a much greater interest, the peace and happiness of your peoples.

If France and England continue to be rivals, the greatest disasters for themselves and for Europe will come of their rivalry. If they unite their interests, as they are already united in political principles and the character of their governments, they will be peaceful and happy, and Europe can hope for peace.

The English nation has nothing more to achieve for her own freedom or greatness; the liberty of all, and the activity of all, is what she should now desire, what she should foster. If she persists in despotism, if she does not renounce her policy of hostility to all prosperity in others . . ., well, we know how Europe punished France for an ambition which was less tyrannical.

Bk. I.

THE BEST FORM OF GOVERNMENT:
PROOF THAT THE PARLIAMENTARY
FORM IS THE BEST

Ch. I

ARGUMENT OF THIS WORK

AFTER a violent convulsion Europe fears fresh disasters, and feels the need for a long repose; the sovereigns of all the European nations are assembled to give her peace. All of them seem to desire peace, all are famed for their wisdom, yet they will not reach their goal. I have asked myself why all the efforts of the statesmen are powerless against the evils which afflict Europe, and I have perceived that there is no salvation for Europe except through a general reorganization. I have thought out a plan of reorganization: the explanation of this plan is the subject of this work.

First, I shall establish the principles on which the organization of Europe should rest; then I shall apply these principles, and finally I shall point out how existing circumstances make it possible for a start to be made in carrying out this plan. Thus the first part will necessarily be somewhat abstract, the second less than the first, the third even less, since the discussion in this part will be solely on events which are taking place before our eyes, in which we are all actors or spectators.

Ch. II

The Congress

A congress is now assembled at Vienna. What will it do? What can it do? That is what I wish to examine. The aim of this congress is to re-establish peace between the powers of Europe, by adjusting the claims of each and conciliating the interests of all. Can one hope that this aim will be achieved? I do not think so, and my reasons for so predicting are as follows. None of the members of the congress will have the function of considering questions from a general point of view; none of them will be even authorized to do so. Each of them, delegate of a king or a people, dependent and holding his rights, powers, mission as such, will come prepared to present the particular policy of the power which he represents, and to shew that this plan coincides with the interest of all. On all sides, the particular interest will be put forward as a matter of common interest. Austria will try to argue that it is important for the repose of Europe that she should have a preponderance in Italy, that she should keep Galicia and the Illyrian provinces, that her supremacy in the whole of Germany should be restored: Sweden will demonstrate, map in hand, that it is a law of nature that Norway should be her dependency; France will demand the Rhine and the Alps as natural frontiers; England will claim that she is, by nature, responsible for policing the seas, and will insist that the despotism which she exercises there should be regarded as the unalterable basis of the political system.

These claims, presented with confidence, perhaps in good faith, in the guise of means to ensure the peace of Europe, and sustained with all the skill of the Talleyrands, Metternichs, and Castlereaghs, will not, however, convince anybody. Each proposition will be rejected because nobody, apart from the mover, will see in it the common interest since he cannot see in it his own interest. They will part on bad terms, blaming on each other the lack of success of the assembly: no agreement, no compromise, no peace. Sectional leagues, rival alliances of interests, will throw Europe back into this melancholy state of war from which vain efforts will have been made to rescue her.

That is what the outcome will shew even more clearly; that is what neither good-will, nor wisdom, nor the desire for peace will be able to avoid. Assemble congress after congress, multiply treaties, conventions, compromises, everything you do will lead only to war; you will not abolish it, the most you can do is to shift the scene of it.

Yet the failure of these methods does not enlighten anybody on their weakness. In politics there is a routine which nobody dares to shake off, although experience clamours to us to change our methods. We blame the force of the evil rather than the weakness of the remedy; and we continue to kill each other without knowing when the carnage will finish, without hope of seeing it end Europe is in a restless state— everybody knows it and says it—but what is this state? How did it arise? Has it always been so? Can it be stopped? These questions are still unanswered.

It is the same with political as with social relations; their stability is assured by similar means. With a union of peoples as with a union of individuals, common institutions and an organization are required. Without these everything is decided by force. To seek peace in Europe by means of treaties and congresses is to seek the maintenance of a society by conventions and agreements. In both cases a compelling force is required which will unite wills, concert movement, make interests common and undertakings firm.

It is the fashion to show a disdainful contempt for the centuries called the Middle Ages. We see in them only a time of stupid barbarism, gross ignorance, repellent superstitions, and we do not notice the fact that it is the only time when the political system of Europe had a real foundation and a common organization. I do not deny that the Popes may have been greedy for power, quarrelsome, despotic, more concerned with satisfying their ambition than curbing that of the kings; that the clergy may have joined in the quarrels of princes, and kept the people brutish in order to tyrannize over them with greater impunity. These evils, melancholy results of an age of ignorance, did not extinguish what was beneficial in this institution. As long as it remained there were few wars in Europe and these wars were of

little importance.[1] Hardly had the revolution brought about by Luther
caused the collapse of the political power of the church than Charles V
conceived this idea of universal dominion, which was attempted after
him by Philip II, Louis XIV, Napoleon and the English people; and
there broke forth the religious wars, ending in the Thirty Years'
War, the longest of all wars!

Despite so many striking examples, prejudice has been so strong
that the greatest minds have been unable to combat it. Everybody
dates the political system of Europe from the sixteenth century only;
everybody regards the treaty of Westphalia as the real basis of this
system.

Yet it is sufficient to examine what has happened since this time
to realize that the balance of powers is a completely false conception;
since peace is its aim, and it has produced nothing but wars, and what
wars!

Only two men have seen the evil and come near to the remedy:
they were Henry IV and the Abbé St. Pierre. The one died before he
could realize his plan, which was forgotten after him; the other was
treated as a visionary because he had promised more than he could
perform.

Certainly the idea of linking all the European peoples by means of
a political organization is by no means a dream, since for six centuries
such an order of things existed, and for six centuries wars were fewer
and less terrible.

This is all that the plan of the Abbé de St. Pierre amounts to, stripped
of those grandiose trappings which have made it ridiculous. It was by
means of a federal government common to all the nations of Europe,
that he hoped to establish his impracticable 'perpetual peace'. This
plan, chimerical in its results, imperfect and defective as it was, is,
however, the most powerful conception which has been produced
since the fifteenth century. Good results are only reached after long
trials and many unsuccessful attempts, and the man who first conceives
a good idea is rarely able to give it the finality and precision which it
acquires with time.

The Abbé de St. Pierre's book has been little read and is hardly
known except for the title, and its general reputation as the dream of a
man of good will.

---

[1] The Crusades, the political aim of which was to discourage the Saracens from the
conquest of Europe, were wars of the confederation as a whole against the enemies of its
liberty.

CH. III

ANALYSIS OF 'PERPETUAL PEACE'

THE Abbé de St. Pierre proposed a general confederation of all the sovereigns of Europe, of which the five principal articles should be:

(1) Plenipotentiaries, nominated by the contracting sovereigns, should assemble at an agreed place and form there a permanent congress.

(2) The number of those sovereigns who should have a vote in the Diet should be defined, and the number of those who should be asked to adhere to the treaty.

(3) The possession of his territory should be guaranteed to each member of the league; his person, family, and powers should be guaranteed against external attack or rebellion of his subjects.

(4) The Diet should be supreme judge of the rights of the members; the interests of each should be determined by arbitration.

(5) Any member of the league who infringed the treaty should be proscribed by Europe and treated as a public enemy. Joint military action at the common expense should be taken against a proscribed state.

The first defect of such a confederation is that it is absolutely impracticable; all the weaknesses of a congress remain untouched. There is no agreement without a common point of view. Can sovereigns negotiating together, or plenipotentiaries nominated by the contracting powers and revocable by them, have any but particular points of view or any interest but their own? If the Court of Rome was able to curb the ambition of the temporal powers, it was because all the members of this Court had a common interest, that of their supremacy over all other courts; it was because the kings did not nominate the Pope or his council, and no power was able to depose him. Henry IV, in his Christian republic, thought he had avoided this difficulty by a simple clause which laid down that each power should put first the interests of the community, and not forward his private interests until after the common interest had been satisfied. Henry IV was a noble character; he thought that what was easy for him should be easy for everybody; but perhaps, in succumbing himself, he would have shewn how good faith in a king is unable to resist the temptations of power. Only by relying on hard facts could one ensure that the organ of the community put common interests first—but I feel that I anticipate, and digress too far. I must return to the analysis which I have begun.

The first result of the constitution of the Abbé de St. Pierre (assuming that it were possible at all), would be to perpetuate the *status quo* in Europe at the moment it was set up. Thenceforward the remnants of feudalism still in existence would become indestructible. Moreover, it would encourage the abuse of power by making the power of sovereigns more dangerous to their peoples, and depriving them of any resource against tyranny. In a word, this sham organization would be nothing but a mutual guarantee of princes to preserve their arbitrary power.

As the lever was first used before the theory of the lever was understood, so there have been national and political organizations, before the nature of such an organization was understood. In politics, as in every science, the right things have been done before the reasons for them have been explained, and when the theory has arrived after the practice, the conception has often been inferior to what has been achieved by chance.

Such is the case here. The organization of Europe, as it was in the fourteenth century, is infinitely superior to the project of the Abbé de St. Pierre. [Every political organization, like every social organization, has its fundamental principles which are its essential nature, without which it cannot live nor produce the desired results.

The principles on which the papal organization was founded have been ignored by the Abbé de St. Pierre. They can be reduced to four:

(1) Any political organization founded to link together several different peoples, while preserving their national independence, must be systematically homogeneous—that is to say, all the institutions should be derived from a single conception, and consequently the government, in all its stages, should have the same form.

(2) The common government must certainly be independent of the national governments.

(3) The members of the common government should be obliged by their position to have a common point of view, and consider exclusively the common interest.

(4) They should be endowed with a power which is their own, and does not derive from any outside authority; this power is public opinion.

The papal organization was founded on these principles, and it is these which made it effective; but the ignorance of the age did not allow these principles to be well applied, and it is this which has vitiated it.

In the first place, the feudal constitution was applied both to the common government and to the national governments, and this constitution is essentially bad, because it acts wholly to the advantage of the rulers and the detriment of the ruled. Secondly, the Popes often used their power, which, like that of the kings, was too absolute, to keep Europe in turmoil instead of making it peaceful.

Finally, public opinion, which was the strength of the common government, was riddled with superstitions, with the result that the Church, in order to maintain its power, had to maintain those superstitions and hinder the progress of enlightenment.

Having reached this point, there is only one further step to take in order to arrive at the best constitution for a league of peoples. It is sufficient to add to the principles already established the three following conditions:

(1) The best possible constitution should be applied to the common government and the national governments.

(2) The members of the common government should be compelled by the nature of the organization to work for the common good. This condition is included in the first.

(3) The intellectual basis of their power should rest on unshakeable principles valid for all times and places.

Ch. IV

The best possible Constitution

I wish to enquire if there is a form of government good in itself, founded on certain, absolute, universal principles, independent of time and place. If I were to try and solve this problem in the way political questions have hitherto been treated, I should only open up another field for interminable discussions. Leaving aside, therefore, everything that may have been said on this matter, I will rely in the enquiry on two principles only, on which certain proof rests—reason and experience.

Every science, of whatever kind, is nothing but a series of problems to resolve, of questions to analyse, and they do not differ from each other except in the nature of these questions. Thus the method applicable to some of them should be applicable to all, for the very reason that it is applicable to some of them; for this method is an instrument entirely independent of the objects to which it applies and changes nothing in their nature. Moreover, it is from the application of this method that every science derives its certainty: by this it becomes positive, and ceases to be a conjectural science; and this only happens after centuries of vagueness, error and uncertainties.

Hitherto, the method of the sciences of observation has not been introduced into political questions; every man has imported his point of view, method of reasoning and judging, and hence there is not yet any precision in the answers, or universality in the results. The time has come when this infancy of the science should cease, and certainly it is desirable it should cease, for the troubles of the social order arise from obscurities in political theory.

What is the best possible constitution?

If we define as a constitution any system of social order aiming at the common goal, the best will be that in which institutions will be organized and powers distributed in such a way that every question of public interest will be treated in the most thorough and complete manner. Now every question of public interest, by the very fact that it is a question, should be solved by the same methods as any other kind of question.

For the solution of a question of any kind logic offers us two methods, or rather a single method comprising two processes— synthesis and analysis. In the one, the thing to be examined is grasped as a whole or examined *a priori*; in the other, it is broken down and examined in detail, i.e., *a posteriori*. The results obtained by synthesis should be verified by analysis, and conversely the results obtained by analysis should be verified by synthesis; or, in other words, a question is not treated surely or completely unless it has been examined first *a priori* and then *a posteriori*.

Therefore I say that the best constitution is that in which each question of public interest is always examined *a priori* and then *a posteriori*.

Now, in a community the examination of questions of public interest first *a priori* and then *a posteriori*, consists precisely in examining them first in the light of the common interest, and then in the light of the particular interests of the members of the community.

It remains, therefore, only to discover by what device a constitution can be organized in such a way that every question of public interest is always examined in the way I have described. For this purpose the first requirement is to establish two distinct authorities, composed in such a way that the one is obliged to consider matters from the point of view of the common interest of the nation, and the other from the point of view of the particular interests of the individual members.

I call the first, Authority for Common Interests, and the second, Authority for Particular or Local Interests. Each should be given the right to formulate and propose any legislation it considers necessary. Up to this point I have described two authorities working towards the same end but on different lines; but the fundamental condition, which gives force to the constitution, is that none of the decisions of the one authority should be put into force without previously being examined and approved by the other. In this way, every legislative measure formulated in the light of the general interest should be examined in the light of particular interests and conversely: or in other words, to return to the language of logic, every legislative measure formulated *a priori* should be examined *a posteriori*, and conversely.

Only good laws would be made, for none would be passed or put into force until the agreement of the two authorities had proved that it was for the good of the people as well as for individuals: or in other words, no measure would be passed until it had demonstrated to be good and wise by the most rigorous logical methods.

The equality of the two authorities which I have described is the basis of the constitution, and the constitution would be vitiated as soon as one authority predominated over the other: as these questions would be examined only from one point of view, either the common interest being sacrificed to the particular, or the particular to the common interest. It is therefore necessary that a third authority, called a Regulating or Moderating Authority, should be set up to maintain the balance between the other authorities and keep them within their proper limits. This third authority should have the right of examining afresh questions of public interest already examined by the other two, of revising errors, vetoing laws which seem defective, and proposing others, which should then be sent for examination by the first two authorities.

Having thus laid down the principles and the foundations of the constitution, it remains to strengthen it by further arrangements, to regulate its action and ensure its stability. These arrangements which may vary according to time and place should be the first concern of the three constitutional authorities; it is for them to create, alter, and abolish these arrangements. The excellence of a constitution founded on the principles I have just established is as certain, as absolute, and universal as the excellence of a good syllogism. Moreover, let it not be thought that this constitution is one of these impracticable theories, one of those chimerical speculations whose only value is to employ the pens of authors. This constitution exists, has lasted more than a hundred years, and this hundred years of experience comes to the support of pure reason. By means of this constitution, a nation has become free, and the most powerful people of Europe.

Ch. V

The English Constitution

ENGLAND is governed by a Parliament with supreme authority, composed of three distinct powers: the King, House of Commons, House of Lords. What is the nature of these three powers, their functions, their qualities? That is what I now proceed to examine.

The King

One man is more capable than a number of men of attaining a unified view, by which the whole scope of a question can be taken in at a single glance. Therefore, the Authority for Common Interests, if we wish it to be well administered, should be in the hands of a single individual. Because he is interested in the nation's glory and greatness, which is also his own, because he is free from the ties which bind each citizen to a particular part of the State which he prefers to the rest, the King cannot have other than general views, other than general interests, to guide him in his actions. The King has, in legislation, only the right of initiation and veto; but in him alone resides the executive power. The difference between the power which makes the laws and that which executes them is that the former should be divided so that every question of public interest should be completely discussed and analysed, and that the latter should be concentrated in a single point, so that executive action can be unified.

House of Commons

In the same way that a question, to be grasped as a whole, should be examined with the breadth of view of which a single individual is capable, so the attention which allows no detail to escape and weighs them all with equal precision, can belong only to an assembly. The House of Commons is composed of delegates from all the provinces, members of all the corporations in the State, who together represent every kind of local or particular interest. This House has, like the King, the initiative and veto in legislation, and exercises to the full the authority which I have called Authority for Particular Interests, because each of the members is obliged to consider first of all the interest of the province which has elected him, or of the corporation of which he is a member. From this constitutional provision which allows both the King and Commons to participate in the making of law, it follows, as I have said, that no measure of public interest is carried out if it harms the majority of particular interests, and no measure of particular interest is put into force if it is contrary to the common interest.

House of Lords

There was a danger that the King might influence the decisions of the Commons, or the Commons those of the King; a danger that the King and the Commons might deceive themselves as to the true interests of the nation or of individuals, and it was therefore necessary to ensure against error, either deliberate or unconscious.

A body of men, highly esteemed by reason of their birth, public services, or wealth, is placed between the King and the Commons to examine afresh the decisions taken, to balance them, correct them, or propose fresh legislation. They exercise this power which I have called 'Regulating' or 'Moderating.'

Regarded from another point of view, the House of Lords checks, on the part of the King and Commons, this natural tendency of individuals and corporations towards absolute power. It contains them within their limits, because of the interest which the Lords have in preserving the privilege which make them an independent corporate body. Supposing this balance were to be destroyed by the King predominating over the Commons, or the Commons over the King, the State would become either despotic or democratic, and each peer would cease to be a member of the government and forced to descend to the level of a courtier or a subject.

Ch. VI

Continued

It is not enough to establish the constitution on its foundations; it is also necessary to ensure that the foundations cannot be shaken.

The King represents the interests of the State as a whole, in the same way that the Commons represent the interest of every part of the State; in the solution of each question the former starts from a single general principle, the good of the nation; the latter from several particular principles, the interests of individuals.

But the Commons are elective, and the Crown is hereditary. Heredity, which is a guarantee for the people that succession to the throne will not be troubled, is no guarantee that the individual who is placed by birth on the throne is the most worthy to occupy it.

That part of the legislative power which the constitution places in the hand sof the King will be badly administered if the King lacks the talents required for it; if he is unjust, the executive power which he wields will be employed for personal vengeance and arbitrary acts.

To avoid these difficulties the monarchy is divided into two parts, essentially different: one comprising the pomp, magnificence, honour, all the marks of sovereignty, the other covering the administration of business. The first part, handed on by hereditary succession, belongs to the reigning dynasty; the second, essentially elective, belongs to the Prime Minister.

The responsibility of ministers guarantees the people against any abuse of power or bad administration.

By this division of the monarchy, on the one hand honours without power, and on the other power without the honours, all the advantages of hereditary succession and of election are united for the good of the people, without any of the disadvantages inherent in each principle by itself. The Chancellor of the Exchequer is not nominated by the King, but by the nation. The King is obliged to choose the man who has obtained the majority in the House of Commons. The moment that the majority pronounces strongly in somebody's favour, that man is carried into power, and the former minister falls from office, without trouble or dissension.

It is the excellence of the Constitution which produces the excellence of the laws, and good laws in their turn strengthen the constitution. Security of property, freedom of the individual, freedom of speech and writing, which secures a closer communication between the government and the governed, and gives the latter an advisory rôle in the actions of the State—all these laws, the product of a good and healthy organization, strengthen it still more, giving it support which it could not find in itself alone. Apart from these particular features of the English constitution, there are others which I omit, because they are peculiar to the English people. If it is untrue to say, as Montesquieu believed, that each nation needs its own form of government (for there can only be one form of good government, as there is only one form of right reasoning), it is at least true that this universal form needs to be varied according to the customs of those to whom it is applied and the times in which it is established.

CH. VII

Conclusion

THE method of the experimental sciences should be applied to politics— reason and experience are the elements of this method. When, by reasoning, I have inquired what is the best possible constitution, I have arrived at the parliamentary constitution; when I have consulted experience, it has confirmed what reason has proved. During the hundred years since England by successfully carrying through her revolution has established this form of government in its fullest development, has not England grown all the time in prosperity and power? What people is freer and richer internally, greater externally, more skilled in industry, sea-faring and commerce? To what can we attribute this unrivalled power, if not to the English government, which is more liberal, more vigorous, more favourable to happiness and national glory than any other government of Europe?

BK. II

ALL THE NATIONS OF EUROPE SHOULD BE GOVERNED BY NATIONAL PARLIAMENTS, AND SHOULD COMBINE TO FORM A COMMON PARLIAMENT TO DECIDE ON THE COMMON INTERESTS OF THE EUROPEAN COMMUNITY

CH. I

THE NEW ORGANIZATION OF THE EUROPEAN COMMUNITY

I HAVE analysed the old organization of Europe, shewn its advantages and defects, and indicated the means by which its advantages can be preserved and its defects eliminated. I have gone on to shew that there is a form of government good in itself, none other than the parliamentary form of constitution. These results bring us naturally to the following conclusion: that wherever the hierarchic or feudal form of government is replaced by the parliamentary form, this change of itself produces a new, more perfect organization, no longer ephemeral like the old system, because its value does not depend on a particular state of the human mind which changes in the course of time, but on the invariable nature of things.

G

Therefore to sum up what I have said so far:

Europe would have the best possible organization if all the nations composing it were to be governed by parliaments, recognizing the supremacy of a common parliament set above all the national governments and invested with the power of judging their disputes.

I shall not speak here of the setting up of the national parliaments; experience shews what their organization should be. I shall only indicate how the common parliament of Europe could be formed.

CH. II

THE HOUSE OF COMMONS OF THE EUROPEAN PARLIAMENT

ANY man born in a particular country and citizen of a particular State, always acquires through his education, contacts, and the examples which he encounters, a more or less settled habit of looking beyond the limits of his own well-being and of merging his own interests in the interests of the community to which he belongs.

When this habit is strengthened and turned into a definite feeling, a man tends to generalize his interests, that is to say, to see them always embodied in the common interest. This tendency, which sometimes weakens but is never extinguished, is what is called patriotism.

In every national government, if it is a good one, the patriotism which each individual brings with him when he becomes a member of the government, changes into a corporate will, since the essential attribute of a good government is that the interest of the government should also be the interest of the nation. It is this corporate will which is the soul of the government, unifying and correcting all its actions, ensuring that they are directed to the same end, and that they respond to the same impulse.

It is the same with the European government as with the national governments: there cannot be action without a will common to all the members of the government.

Now this corporate will, which in a national government springs from national patriotism, must come in the European government from a greater breadth of view, a wider sentiment, which we may call European patriotism.

Montesquieu says that institutions mould men. Therefore this tendency which fosters a patriotism beyond the limits of one's own fatherland, this habit of considering the interests of Europe instead of national interests, will be a natural development among those who compose the European parliament, once it is established.

This is true, but it is also the fact that men make institutions, and an institution cannot take root if men are not adapted for it beforehand, or at least in a condition to be adapted.

It is therefore essential to admit to the House of Commons of the European Parliament, i.e. one of the two active powers of the European constitution, only such men as by their wide contacts, emancipation from purely local customs, their occupations which are cosmopolitan in aim rather than national, are better able to arrive quickly at this wider point of view which makes the corporate will, and at the common interest which should be also the corporate interest of the European parliament.

Men of business, scientists, magistrates, and administrators are the only classes who should be summoned to form the House of Commons of the great parliament. It is a fact that whatever common interests exist in the European community can be traced to the sciences, arts, law, commerce, administration, and industry.

For every million persons in Europe who know how to read and write there should sit as their representatives in the House of Commons of the great parliament, a man of business, a scientist, an administrator and a lawyer. Thus, assuming that there are sixty million men in Europe who know how to read and write, the House will be composed of 240 members. The election of members will be made by the professional body to which they belong. They will be elected for ten years. Every member of the House must possess 25,000 francs income at least, from landed property.

It is true that property makes for stable government, but it is only when property is not divorced from enlightenment that government can be safely placed on such a basis. It is right, therefore, that the government should co-opt and endow with property those who are without property but distinguished by outstanding merit, in order that talent and property should not be divided. For talent, which is the more powerful and active force, would soon seize on property if the two were not united.

Therefore, at each fresh election, twenty members chosen from among the most distinguished men of learning, men of business, lawyers and administrators, who are not landed proprietors, should be admitted to the House of Commons of the European parliament, and endowed with 25,000 francs income from landed property.

Ch. III

The House of Peers

JUST as every peer of a national parliament should have outstanding wealth in his own country, so the peers of the European parliament should have wealth which makes them outstanding in the whole of Europe. Every peer of Europe should possess at least 500,000 francs income from landed property. The peers would be nominated by the King, without limitation of numbers. Peerage would be hereditary. There should be twenty members of the House of Peers chosen from men, or the descendants of men, who by their work in the sciences, industry, law or administration, have performed the greatest services to the European community. These members should be endowed by the European parliament with 500,000 francs income from landed property. Apart from the twenty nominated at the beginning, one new peer should be nominated and endowed at each renewal of parliament.

Ch. IV

The King

THE choice of the head of the European community is of such importance, and requires such careful consideration, that I postpone discussion of it for a second work which will appear later, as the sequel to this work.

The King of the European parliament should be the first to take up his office, and to carry through the formation of the two Houses; action must begin with him, so that the setting up of the great parliament is accomplished without revolution and disorders. The monarchy should be hereditary.

Ch. V

Internal and external action of the great Parliament

EVERY question of common interest of the European community should be brought before the great parliament, to be considered and decided by it. It should be the sole judge of disputes arising between the different governments.

If a particular part of the European population, under a particular government, wishes to form a separate nation, or to come under another government, it is for the European parliament to decide the issue. It will decide, not in the interests of the governments, but of the peoples, bearing in mind always the best possible organization of the European Confederation.

The European parliament should have a city and surrounding territory as its property in full sovereignty.

The parliament will have the right to levy from the Confederation such taxes as may be considered necessary.

All undertakings of common advantage to the European community will be directed by the great parliament; thus, for instance, it will link the Danube to the Rhine by canals, the Rhine to the Baltic, etc. Without external activity, there is no internal tranquillity. The surest means of maintaining peace in the Confederation will be to keep it constantly occupied beyond its own borders, and engaged without pause in great internal enterprises. To colonize the world with the European race, superior to every other human race; to make the world accessible and habitable like Europe—such is the sort of enterprise by which the European parliament should continually keep Europe active and healthy.

State education in the whole of Europe will be under the direction and supervision of the great parliament.

A code of general as well as national and individual ethics will be drawn up by the great parliament, to be taught throughout Europe. It will demonstrate that the principles on which the European Confederation rests are the best, the most solid, the only principles capable of making the community as happy as it can be, according to the nature of man, and the state of his enlightenment. The great parliament will allow complete freedom of conscience, and of worship; but it will prohibit religions with principles contrary to the great moral code which will have been drawn up. Thus the European peoples will be united by the essential bonds in any political association; uniformity of institutions, union of interests, conformity of principles, a common ethic and a common education.

CH. VI

CONCLUSION

THIS book would require the longest development and the reason is obvious. I shall not prolong it now, in order not to keep the reader from important points by dwelling on details which would take too much time to discuss further.

Bk. III

FRANCE AND ENGLAND, WHICH HAVE A PARLIAMENTARY FORM OF
GOVERNMENT, SHOULD FORM A COMMON PARLIAMENT EMPOWERED TO
CONTROL THE INTERESTS OF BOTH NATIONS. EFFECT OF THE ANGLO-
FRENCH PARLIAMENT ON THE OTHER EUROPEAN PEOPLES

Ch. I

*Foundation of the European Parliament: how it can de done as soon as
possible*

MEN may fail for a long time to realize their own advantage, but the
time comes when they are enlightened and act accordingly. The
French have adopted the English constitution, and all the peoples of
Europe will adopt it gradually, as they become sufficiently enlightened
to appreciate its advantages. Now the time when all the European
peoples are governed by national parliaments will unquestionably be
the time when a common parliament can be established without
difficulties. The reasons for this proposition are so evident that it
seems to me pointless to enumerate them.

But this time is still far off, and frightful wars and repeated revolutions will afflict Europe in the meantime. What is to be done to avert
these new evils, the melancholy results of the disorganization in which
Europe still remains? We must use our intelligence, and find means of
abolishing the causes of these evils, with less delay.

I return to what I have already said. The establishment of the
European parliament will be brought about without difficulty as soon
as all the peoples of Europe live under a parliamentary régime. It
follows that the European parliament can begin to take shape as soon as
that part of the European population governed by a representative
régime is superior in force to that which remains subject to arbitrary
government.

Now this state of affairs is precisely what exists at present: the
English and the French are unquestionably superior in power to the
rest of Europe, and the English and the French have a parliamentary
form of government. It is therefore possible to begin at once on the
reorganization of Europe. Let the English and the French join together
and establish a common parliament: let the principal aim of this association be to grow by attracting to it other peoples; consequently, let
the Anglo-French government encourage among all the other nations
the supporters of a representative constitution; let them back them

with all their power, in order that parliaments can be established of the peoples subject to absolute monarchies, and let every nation, as soon as it has adopted the representative form of government, join the association and nominate representatives of her own to the common parliament. Thus the organization of Europe will be achieved gradually without wars, catastrophes, or political revolutions.

CH. II

THE ANGLO-FRENCH PARLIAMENT

THE composition of the Anglo-French parliament should be the same as that which I have suggested for the great European parliament. The French will have only a third of the representatives: that is to say, England should provide two deputies and France one for each million men who are literate.

This condition is important for two reasons; firstly, because the French are still inexperienced in parliamentary politics and need to be under the guidance of the English, who are trained and experienced; secondly, because in agreeing to the establishment of this body England would be making in some ways a sacrifice, whereas France can gain from it nothing but advantage.

CH. III

IT is to the interest of France and England to unite in a political association. The union of France and England can lead to the re-organization of Europe. This union, hitherto impracticable, is now possible because France and England have the same political principles and the same form of government. But is the mere possibility sufficient to bring about a reform? Certainly not; it still needs the will to do it.

England and France are each threatened with a great political upheaval and neither can by itself find means to avert it. Both will inevitably trip up if they do not mutually support each other. By a strange and fortunate coincidence, the only resource which they have against an inevitable revolution is this union which will increase the prosperity of both and put an end to the misfortunes of Europe.

CH. IV

ANALYSIS OF THE CONDITION OF ENGLAND

THE division between the party in office and the opposition is not the only division in public opinion. This is only a part of a greater, older, and permanent division of the nation into two parties, Whigs and Tories.

The Tories have constantly been in the majority, and therefore in office, and consequently the present situation of England is the result of their work. Let us glance at the position of England. She has destroyed and eliminated any fleet which might, by joining with another, rival her own fleet. Command of the sea is certainly in her hands. She dominates Asia and Africa. She leaves the Spanish and the Portuguese the expense and trouble of governing South America, while she takes the profits. She has deprived the North Americans of any possibility of rivalling her in commerce.

By means of the balance of Europe, which she has learnt to manipulate, nothing takes place on the Continent against her will; she spreads peace or war there as she pleases. The commerce of the whole world is in her hands; she surpasses every other nation in agriculture and in industry. Thus the influence of England on the rest of the human race is the most widespread, the greatest, and the most astonishing, known to history: England has reached the height of glory and power.

But the total debt of England is far greater than the value of the land of the three kingdoms together—hence an unnatural state of affairs. This unnatural state of affairs has led to a considerable rise in price of essential commodities, which in turn raises the cost of labour, and hence inevitably the price of manufactured goods. Paper money loses in value against gold, and the exchange is constantly disadvantageous.

The patriotism of the English people, as long as it was threatened by Bonaparte, has given the government the means to bear the enormous burden, but can it continue to bear it in the calm of a period of peace? Undoubtedly not: if a remedy is not promptly applied a revolution in the financial system, and a political revolution, will be inevitable. This revolution will come all the sooner because it will be excited by the Whigs, as the only means of making their principles prevail and seizing the helm. Let us consider the Whigs.

The Whigs strongly opposed the American War. They thought that Great Britain should unhesitatingly grant to its Continental subjects of the New World the independence which they asked as a favour, but knew they could win by conquest if it was refused to them. None of the Whigs has condoned the despotism, injustice, and atrocities of the English government in India. From the beginning of the French revolution, and throughout its course, the Whigs constantly maintained that the English nation should declare itself in favour of the party working for the transformation of the social system of France and the establishment of a representative constitution. When Burke and the Tories burst into invective and made England echo with the famous phrase 'The French have passed beyond liberty,' the Whigs retorted 'Has not mankind owed its greatest political advances to the most violent crises and most bloody upheavals? Did not our own ancestors have their moments of madness and fury, like the French? Did they not too soil their hands with the blood of their innocent king? Were our Levellers less absurd, less inimical to every social principle than the Jacobins, and was Cromwell less of a tyrant than Bonaparte? Yet it was our revolution, so similar to the French Revolution, which made us what we are; by it the English people is free at home and powerful abroad. Do not doubt that whatever efforts we make to decry and oppose this revolution, the French will in the long run derive from it the advantages we have got from our own; they will be free and great as we are. Let us protect them now that they are weak, and our help can save them from the evils which still threaten them.'

Finally, the Whigs have constantly preached this principle that the liberty of Great Britain will be the more complete and the more secure, as the peoples of the continent become more free. They have constantly told the Tories: 'You are making vain efforts to halt the progress of enlightenment in the nations of Europe which nothing can stop. The huge cost which this attempt involves will not bring success and will increase the national debt to a total which will make it impossible to pay off the capital or even pay the interest. The debt will create a class of fictitious fortunes which will raise the price of food, which in turn will increase wages, and hence in turn the price of manufactured goods. The increasing cost of manufactured goods will increase imports and decrease exports, resulting in the increase of expenditure and fall in revenue; when finally the State cannot pay the interest on the Debt, bankruptcy will be inevitable.'

Events have taught the English people that the Whigs were right; they begin to feel the need to change their foreign policy,

But why have the Tories constantly kept a majority and prevailed over the Whigs?

Why has the ministry and consequently the conduct of affairs hitherto been in their hands? Will it remain so, and for how long?

A secret instinct tells the English that their liberty would be in danger if they had close relations with peoples who were still not sufficiently enlightened to live under a liberal régime. Thus the Tories, who admired the despotism and isolation of England, were bound to obtain the majority of votes since their opinion coincided with the interests of the people.

When Bonaparte alarmed England by his vast and insensate plan of universal dominion, all parties became silent; each citizen ceased to be Whig or Tory and became simply an Englishman. Every opinion was swallowed up by a single aim, the need to save the country. But now that England can, without fear, ally herself with France since France has the same constitution as herself, now that the country, free from danger, allows the citizens the leisure to weigh the opinions of the two parties, which of them will be carried into power?

Every Englishman whose political opinion is of any weight is a creditor of the State for a greater or less sum, and therefore personally interested in the fulfilment by the State of its obligations. Thus all the members of the Whig party will be impelled on the one hand by the desire to gain power, and on the other by the desire to prevent the bankruptcy of the State. Now that they see that bankruptcy is bound to follow from a political movement which will bring them into power, their political opinion will be balanced by their personal interest, and they will remain quiet and let things slide from fear of injuring their interests if they try to oppose them.

It follows, therefore, that the Tories will remain in power, and will remain there as long as they are still able to raise loans; and, faithful to their old system, they will try and foment trouble in France in order to prevent the development of industry there. It is, however, easy to see that the time will come when the English government will be forced to confess to the people that the interest of the debt can no longer be paid, and then, by a political upheaval, power will pass from the Tories to the Whigs.

What we need to know is whether there is a means of avoiding the bankruptcy of England and making the government abandon its foreign policy for a more liberal policy, i.e. of transferring the government from the Tories to the Whigs without revolution or bankruptcy. I believe this to be possible, but it is not in herself that England can find the means, she must seek it outside; it can only come from an association with France. England can be compared to a great commercial firm which has built magnificent capital equipment, but at the cost of an enormous debt. If she finds a rich partner she will prosper; if she fails to do so she will inevitably go bankrupt. Not only has England need of France, but France also has need of England, and both have an equal interest urging them to unite.

CH. V

ANALYSIS OF FRENCH POLITICS

IT is not through political caprice or unforeseen chance that France has adopted the English constitution; more than a hundred years of effort have prepared her for it. The authority of the Pope, the unlimited power of the kings, the privileges of the nobility and the clergy, the wealth which sustained their power, were so many obstacles which had to be removed before France could be reorganized. Public opinion was the first step to the destruction of these powers which had been created by public opinion, and this step was the work of the eighteenth century. The church was ridiculed, arbitrary authority made odious, and the nobility brought into contempt.

The Encyclopedia, the result of the work of the whole century, dealt the decisive blow by overthrowing altogether the inherited prejudices, the traditional fallacies which upheld the old order. The revolution, prepared by the writers, was hastened by the American war. The ideas of liberty and of free institutions, the hatred of tyranny in any form which the defenders of the United States brought back from their intercourse with a free but oppressed people, soon took hold of a considerable part of the nation, and the crisis began. The rights of the throne, the power of the nobility and clergy, already weakened at their roots, put up only a weak resistance. Their wealth was seized, their persons proscribed, even the King was not spared. Louis XVI loved his people, he had everything to make him a good king; but even Titus would have fallen, like him, if Titus had reigned in his place. The firmness which he lacked would no more have served him than his weakness. It was not the prince but the throne which was attacked; the accident of birth brought him to the throne, which involved him in its fall.

All the enthusiasm, the madness, the horrors of the French Revolution are paralleled in the English Revolution. In both the aim was the same; in both the same events led up to it, so true is it that the progress of the human mind is invariable and does not change according to time or place. The similarity is such that it is possible to pick out at once the common element in the two revolutions, and apply it to each of them in turn. Both were divided into five stages distinguished according to the character of the events.

First Period

The progress of enlightenment reveals the anomalies of the old social order, and makes the need of a new organization felt. The desire to bring about this change for the better takes hold of every one. The King, the nobles, the people all wish to take part in it: there is only one aim, one tendency, one desire, the public welfare. Every one is resolved to achieve it at whatever price; private interests disappear before the interest of all.

Second Period

The glamour fades; they hesitate in face of the sacrifices which, at a distance, appeared insignificant; they repent of their rash enthusiasm. The burning, ecstatic, blind love for the public welfare becomes calmer and more considered; advantages and losses are weighed. Some hanker after the old order, and rouse themselves to check the progress of the new order and oppose its supporters. The reformers seek support for the populace, and stir them up; popular societies are formed.

Third Period

As power passes into the hands of the most ignorant class, administration is bad, anarchy appears, civil war and famine complete the disaster.

Fourth Period

When the disorder is at its height, weariness brings a desire to return to order and discipline; the despotism of a single man appears less objectionable than the despotism of the people. Whoever dares to seize power is certain to be accepted. Then a bold and ambitious man, a Cromwell or a Bonaparte, emerges from the crowd; armed with a strong will, and backed by the public demand, he snatches power from the mob and gathers it in his own hands. As military force alone can destroy the power of the people, a military despotism is built up on the ruins of democratic anarchy.

Fifth Period

When calm returns after such upheavals the changes desired at the beginning by the moderate part of the nation are brought into effect without difficulty, and the nation sees at last the social order which it hoped to achieve without convulsions and disorders.

Such is the history of the English and of the French revolution, briefly summarized.

I leave it to the reader to verify this analysis in regard to the former; as to the latter, which of us who has reached the age of fifty, has not retained sharply contrasting recollections: first, of the brave days of the National Assembly, then of the follies of the Legislative Assembly, then the atrocities of the Convention? Which of us has not felt ashamed of the tyranny from which France has been delivered, and has not felt moved to rejoice at seeing the descendants of Louis XII and Henry IV bring back to us after a long exile both the virtues of their ancestors and institutions which conform to our enlightenment?

It is the same with a series of events as with a series of numbers when there are four terms common to both series, they will continue so indefinitely. If we consider the revolutions of France and England as two series, they have five similar terms, and the fifth term of the French revolution is the present state of affairs.

It is possible to say with certainty that if there was a sixth term in the English revolution, there will be a similar sixth term, corresponding to it, in the French revolution. The sixth term in the English revolution was the expulsion of the Stuarts.

A catastrophe of this sort would be dreadful for France, and yet we are threatened with it through the force of events. It is no use deluding ourselves and refusing to look at the impending future; we must stop it, and eliminate it, and that cannot be done without thinking about it.

CH. VI

CAUSES OF A NEW REVOLUTION IN FRANCE

There used to be in France a privileged caste to which all the honours and important posts belonged. The nobility, doubled in number by Bonaparte, is now divided into two parties opposed to each other; both are discontented. The old nobility, accustomed to regard all the great offices of State as their patrimony, are indignant, seeing a mass of new men sitting in the places occupied by their ancestors. The new nobility, proud of their wealth, managing their offices with ability, since they held them before they were ennobled, base their claims on their intelligence, while the old nobility base their claims on birth. The new nobility are irritated at seeing the posts which they feel they alone are fit to hold, given to men who have grown old without experience of government, in idleness or exile.

It is in the military class, which has always been foremost in France, that this struggle between the old and the new men is most obvious. The officers who served under Bonaparte, mostly reduced to half-pay, after so many labours and success, feel it bitterly when they see new formations appearing every day, the leaders of which have not shared their labours or their victories. Above all, their chief complaint is that the Household Guard, covered in gold lace, but still without glory or experience of war, has been put above the Old Guard which made Europe tremble. On their side the old nobility claim all the military posts. They consider they have been illegally deprived both of the posts which they have lost, and the posts which they never held; they demand what they held before, and also what they might have had. Amid all these opposing interests, and rival claims, there is a general clamour; regret for the past and discontent at the present.

If we turn from the highest class of society to the next class, we see first of all the magistrates and all the related professions humiliated because they have lost their political importance and the great names which adorned it. If the judiciary could not expect to see its former prerogatives revived, at least it might have hoped to see the highest judges sitting in Parliament, as in England.

The commercial, banking, business, manufacturing class need a bank which is secure and independent of the government, encouragement for industry, and recognition for those who distinguish themselves there. This class, so important for the power of the State, is still crushed by the pretentions and the prestige of the nobility.

In the class of have-nots there is nothing but complaints against the consolidated excise in which the method of collection recalls the most hateful tyranny.

The inhabitants of the ports and coasts of France complain that they are reduced to a coasting-trade only and cannot find an outlet for their activities by developing ocean commerce, because of the loss of our most important colonies and of the despotism of the English.

All classes of society, all Frenchmen, are indignant at the feebleness of the government in giving up Belgium; they are resentful when they see Austria increased by a part of Poland and the Illyrian provinces, Russia by Crimea, Finland, and vast areas in Asia, Prussia by Silesia and a part of Poland, while France is humiliated, weakened, and reduced to her old frontiers.

Cн. VII

Continued

THE complaints in all classes of the nation caused by frustrated interests and disappointed hopes combine against the government, which has not acted either firmly or frankly.

In the twenty-five years which have elapsed since France overthrew the old order, ten constitutions have been in turn adopted and discarded. These experiments, marked by terrible atrocities due to the fury of party strife, have been, so to speak, the stages by which we have travelled from the old order to the present one. The representative constitution in which the exhausted nation rests to-day seems to be the fulfilment of our wishes, and should be so since it is the best form of government. There is no longer reason to fear a revolutionary change in the constitution, for the constitution is firmly established in public opinion; and if we are threatened with a political upheaval it will not be on the constitutional provisions, but on those who operate them, that the blows will fall. Every action of the French parliament since its establishment has displeased the majority of the people. It has been equally feeble and clumsy both in national and foreign policy. It was hoped that its first care would be to secure liberty of the press, liberty of the individual, responsibility of ministers—things which are the only guarantees for the governed against oppression.

Let us turn from parliament as a whole to an analysis of the three powers of which it is composed.

Apart from a small number of men, whose names have become so famous that it is unnecessary for me to mention them here, the deputies, used to servitude under the tyranny of Bonaparte, have not the courage to believe that they cannot be anything more than instruments to be used at will. There are supporters of absolute power in the House of Commons of the French parliament; men who owe their entire position to the constitution, turn against it the power which they derive from the constitution; by a strange preference they would rather be the clients of a minister than members of one of the legislative bodies.

The same courage in a handful of men who know their powers and use them properly, the same weakness in the majority who allow themselves to be led, appear in the Peers. This house, having not yet acquired a hereditary character, is entirely under the power of the King.

The lack of precision in execution, the disorder in the Government's views, produced by the difference of opinion in the two houses on constitutional points, is aggravated by the King. Inoculated against any idea of absolute authority by his character and his philosophic principles, he is yet forced back to it in spite of himself by ingrained habits of his childhood, and by the advice of his entourage. On the one hand his wisdom suggests the answer, but his education calls him back; in the struggle of equal forces, pushing against each other, the King hesitates, is uncertain, is contradictory, and his decisions reflect the incoherence of his motives. It is this uncertainty in the whole parliament, wavering between an order of things which has been destroyed and cannot be restored, and another order which is coming but not yet consolidated, that gives rise to mistakes and complaints.

It is anomalous to try and reconcile what is irreconcilable. What else are they trying to do, when, by a bizarre mixture of arbitrary and representative government, they have a King who is at the same time absolute and constitutional; deputies who are clients of absolute ministers, peers who are slaves of the King's will? A mongrel form of government in which representation is nothing but a sham façade without any effect on the abuse of power—that is what we see to-day. This confusion of the two systems which cannot exist together, although they try to keep them in step, is due to one cause, the lack of experience of those who operate the constitution.

If the same step which brought parliamentary government into being in France had destroyed in men's minds the habits formed under the preceding government, and given everyone sound ideas on the social system, less complaints would have been raised now, and we should be threatened with fewer evils. Time, no doubt, and experience, will teach those who govern us, but the remedy is slow, the evils urgent, experience belated.

If we remark that the English government is still in the hands of the Tories, and that the Tories, after having exhausted in vain their efforts to prevent the French nation from reaching its present position, now seek to turn it back and hamper the work of a weak and tottering government, we shall realize that France is seated on a volcano, the explosion of which will be the more terrible the longer it is delayed.

Ch. VIII

Trend of the Revolution

The discontent of the nation, the intrigues of England, the weakness of the government, threaten France with revolution at an early date.

On whom will the blow from this revolution fall? On the deputies? As the deputies are only elected for a period, a revolution could only take away from them a power which they could not hope to keep permanently, but may hope to recover. On the Peers? The peerage is not yet hereditary, and any peer may cease to be a peer without his social position being destroyed. On the King? Here it is quite different; the monarchy is hereditary, the throne is the only property, the only existence for the royal family.

Therefore, this revolution which is not a threat to the two Houses, would fall with all its weight on the King and his family: the reason for this alarming catastrophe is that monarchy in France is not yet divided.[1]

If the administrative aspect of the monarchy was separated from the hereditary aspect, a political shock would only affect the administrative powers; the blow would fall on the ministers alone and would not reach the King. But, as both powers are concentrated in the same place, the one cannot be struck without the other.

The responsibility of ministers is the surest and strongest safeguard of the dynasty.

To-day, owing to habits surviving from the old order, a part of the nation attributes everything to the King, makes him the centre of everything, the motive power of everything, and regards other authorities as merely emanating from the royal power. This belief which should have been carefully destroyed, and has been kept alive by the love of the French for their King because they like to think they obey the prince they love, is fatal to the King's interests and to the dynasty, and likely to concentrate against the dynasty the whole weight of the coming revolution. It is against the King who is regarded as the cause of everything that complaints are directed, against him who is held responsible for all evils that all mistakes are held. If this unfortunate position was without a remedy, I would have

---

[1] See Bk. I, ch. v.

kept silence in order not to torture France to no purpose by foretelling an inevitable disaster; but we are not yet reduced to despair. The dangers which threaten us can be averted, and as it is vitally important to show how this can be done, I should have been to blame if I had kept silence.

CH. IX

THE MEANS OF AVOIDING A SECOND REVOLUTION IN FRANCE

I HAVE explained the causes of the revolution which threatens France. However numerous these may be, they can be removed by a single step.

When the national pride of a people is wounded, the irritation of the whole nation affects individuals, and aggravates in each of them the feeling of their own particular wrongs. When this pride is satisfied, particular grievances are submerged in the general feeling of contentment.

As soon as it is politically united to England, the French nation, weakened at the moment, will play a paramount rôle in Europe, and French pride, depressed by the present position of France, will revive. Thus claims will be forgotten, interests combined, personal pride will be satisfied; at least the passions which at present are so strong will be weakened and soon extinguished.

In its relations with the rest of the world, France will share all the advantages enjoyed by England.

The sovereignty of the seas, shared by the French nation, will expand her commerce and industry, develop her shipping which is weak at present; in fact, it hardly exists at all.

Paper money, to make circulation more active, is necessary to stimulate French industry; a bank common to both nations, established by the Anglo-French parliament, would satisfy the wishes of the commercial class in this respect. Finally, public opinion in France would be fixed on a solid basis by close intercourse with the English, our teachers in politics. The parliament of England and the Anglo-French parliament by their influence on the new French parliament, could set it on the true constitutional path, and strengthen the progress of the government, by removing this hesitation which comes from the struggle between old customs and new ideas.

Ch. X

SUMMARY OF VIEWS ON FRANCE AND ENGLAND

I HAVE climbed to the height where one can see the common interest of France and England.

Let those who have followed attentively, who have made the ascent with me, and discovered from there a remedy for the ills of the two nations, descend again to the level of national interests and stratagems which hitherto have been the only ideas, and are still being pursued. What do we see? Rivalries, wars, evils within and without.

England, alarmed at the approach of revolution, intensifies her policy. She schemes in cold blood for new wars in Europe and new disasters in France; she supports the cause of the negro, and ravages the territory of her kinsmen. The whole of Europe is indignant at the news of the burning of Washington. Yet her intrigue, oppression, her crimes at which she herself shudders, but feels compelled to commit, will not save her; at most they can but stave off the crisis.

Consider England as she tries to crush every rising force, beggaring herself to impoverish other nations, weakening herself in the effort to weaken others, as if there was no safety for her except in the misery and ruin of others; consider her, aghast at her own atrocities, contemplating others and bringing on herself the hatred of the whole of humanity, in order to prolong for a short time this unhappy state of agitation and disquiet, of growing fear, which is barely hidden by an appearance of force and of external prosperity.

Think of her, on the other hand, united with France, saved by this union from inevitable bankruptcy, powerful and happy, without crimes or fears, the prosperity of others no longer harming her now— and tell me which of these states is preferable.

France, after the crisis which overturned her old political system, has not yet created a new one.

Let France by a generous gesture regard the national debt of England as the result of the efforts which had to be made to secure a home for liberty in Europe, whence it would spread to all nations; let France agree to share the burden of a sacrifice of which she enjoys the benefits. Let England, with an impulse equally noble, share with France the advantages she has accumulated through a hundred years of liberty.

The huge size of this debt need not alarm either nation. It will steadily decrease, since, as each nation on attaining its liberty joins the Anglo-French community, the debt will be shared with her in proportion to her wealth.

It will therefore be to the interests of the Anglo-French confederation to promote with all its power the reorganization of Europe.

The less we frustrate the interests of others in working for our own, the less resistance we find from them; everybody attains their aim more easily. Thus the hackneyed saying 'We cannot be really happy unless we seek our happiness in the happiness of others' is as certain and positive as the proposition that a body moving in a certain direction is stopped or retarded if it meets other bodies moving in the opposite direction.

Ch. XI

Germany

There is one nation in Europe which seems in its government to be nothing out of the ordinary among European nations, but is infinitely superior in its character, science, and philosophy.

A high standard of morality, a sincerity which never stoops to deceit, an uprightness proof against every temptation, is to be found in the German nation. In the midst of terrible wars, atrocious hatreds, intolerable oppression, this character has not been betrayed. No French soldier was ever killed by treachery in this country which France ravaged.

Deprived almost entirely of sea-going commerce, Germany has been spared the commercial spirit which puts money above the finer feelings, leads to egoism and blindness to what is great and noble. In Germany one does not ask as in England, 'What is that man worth?' Meaning 'What are his possessions?' Merit is not measured by wealth.

It is a remarkable thing that this natural kindliness and simplicity, which is the character of the people extends to the rulers. Arbitrary power in Germany is soft-hearted and paternal. A nation may appear in one of three states, or stages; the first is to cringe under arbitrary government, to enjoy slavery, and conceive of nothing more desirable than the favour of rulers, nothing nobler than the honours granted by them.

The second state is when a people learns how to raise itself above the social system in which it lives by its philosophic enlightenment and nobility of its ideas; to have emancipated itself from ideas of favouritism which can only be gained by base behaviour; to have realized that there is something more worthy of man than that, and aspired to it, fighting against the existing order, but without trying to alter it.

The third state, and certainly the best, is when a people has set up a government in which any one can participate, if he is worthy, and can direct his efforts and intelligence to the maintenance and perfection of the social order. This last state is that which England and France have reached; the second state is that of Germany.

It is fine, no doubt, to raise oneself to the level of the noblest sentiments in the midst of base servitude; to escape from the limitations of absolute despotism by means of the freedom conferred by pure thought; but it is finer, I think, to achieve the creation of a free government, which one can enjoy without baseness or shame.

Germany has advanced beyond her social system, but has left it still intact: England and France have raised themselves, and have also raised their governments to their own level.

CH. XII

GERMANY is now in a great state of agitation.

Ideas of liberty sprout everywhere; everywhere it is apparent that a revolution is impending.

The memory of the English Revolution, the more recent memory of the French Revolution alarm the German nation. They refuse to believe that they are confronted with such evils, and hope that their character will preserve them. They deceive themselves. National character cannot avail against the force of events, and that is the position in this case. There is no change in the social order without a change in property. Enthusiasm for the public welfare may at first produce agreement to the sacrifices required—that is the first stage of the revolution; but soon there are regrets and resistance—that is the second stage. The resistance of the property-owners cannot be overcome unless the have-nots are armed; hence civil war, proscription, massacre.

What can save a nation from these disasters? Nothing, except protection from outside for the supporters of the new social order, which holds in check the property-owners opposed to the revolution. The disasters of the English Revolution were inevitable, for there was no power in Europe to support the establishment of a free government.

France could have been saved by England; England refused her help. Far from extinguishing the conflagration, she sought to increase it;

France was drowned in blood. Germany to-day is in the position of England and France then; the same evils threaten her, the same help could save her.

Moreover, conditions peculiar to Germany would increase the violence of her revolution; she has further to go than England or France. Not only must she change her constitution, she must also unite, and centralize in one government, a mass of separate governments. A divided Germany is at the mercy of the whole world; only through unity can she become powerful. The first undertaking of the Anglo-French parliament should be to promote the reorganization of Germany, by making her revolution shorter and less violent.

The German nation, by virtue of its population which comprises half the population of Europe, of its central position, above all of its noble and generous character, is destined to play the paramount part in Europe, as soon as it has been united under a free government.

When the time has arrived at which the Anglo-French community can be enlarged by the addition of Germany, when a common parliament for the three nations has been established, the reorganization of the rest of Europe will be quicker and easier; for the Germans who are nominated to the common parliament will contribute in their views that pureness of morality, nobility of sentiments which distinguishes them, and will raise to their level, by example, the English and French, who are by reason of their commercial pursuits more egoistic and less disinterested. In this way, the principles of the parliament will become more liberal, their actions more disinterested, their policy more favourable to other nations.

Conclusion

I HAVE tried in this work to prove that the establishment of a political system in conformity with the present state of enlightenment, and the creation of a common power possessing force enough to repress the ambitions of peoples and kings, is the only means of producing a stable and peaceful order in Europe. In this respect the actual plan of organization which I have suggested is of secondary importance; if it were refuted, if it were found to be essentially faulty, I would still have done what I set out to do, provided some other plan were adopted.

From another point of view, the plan I have suggested is the most important part of my work. For a long time it has been agreed that the present political system is decayed to its very foundations, and that another system must be set up.

Yet in spite of the fact that this view is widespread, and that men's minds, wearied by revolutions and wars, are prepared to grasp at any means to recover order and repose, nobody has risen above the old routine. They have continued to act on the old principles, as if it was impossible to have any better ones; they have rung the changes on the old system in a thousand different ways, but nothing new has been thought of. The plan of organization which I have put forward is the first which is new and comprehensive.

Doubtless it would have been desirable that the plan of re-organization of the European community should have been thought out by one of the more powerful sovereigns, or at least by a statesman experienced in affairs and renowned for his political talent. Such a plan, backed by great power, or a great reputation, would have converted men's minds more quickly. The feebleness of human intelligence did not allow matters to follow this course. Was it possible for those who are engaged in the day-to-day conduct of affairs, and forced inevitably to reason according to the principles of the old system, which they maintain for lack of a better one, to pursue simultaneously two different courses? With their attention fixed on the old system and the old devices, could they conceive and keep before their eyes a new system and new methods?

With great effort and labour I have reached the standpoint of the common interest of the European peoples. This standpoint is the only one from which it is possible to perceive both the evils which threaten us, and the means of averting them. If those who are in charge of affairs can reach the same level as I have done, they will all be able to see what I have seen. The divisions of public opinion arise from the fact that each man has too narrow a view, and does not dare to free himself from this standpoint from which he persists in judging affairs.

For clear-thinking men there is only one method of reasoning, only one way of seeing things, if they are looking at them from the same point of view. If men who have the same nobility of sentiment, uprightness of judgment, desire for the public welfare, loyalty to the King, yet have such different opinions, it is because each has his own point of view which he will not abandon.

Let them rise above it, and put themselves in the position to which

I have tried to elevate men's minds, and all these different opinions will merge into one.

Thus by a happy transformation, beneficial to the State, we shall see all the finest characters, the most enlightened minds, the Montesquious and the Raynouards, the d'Ambrais and the Lanjuinais, and all the others separated by their opinions but united by their feelings, aiming at the same goal and co-operating for the same purpose. There will come a time, without doubt, when all the peoples of Europe will feel that questions of common interest must be dealt with before coming down to national interests; then evils will begin to lessen, troubles abate, wars die out. That is the ultimate direction in which we are steadily progressing; it is there that the progress of the human mind will carry us. But which is more worthy of man's prudence—to hasten towards it, or to let ourselves be dragged there?

Poetic imagination has put the Golden Age in the cradle of the human race, amid the ignorance and brutishness of primitive times; it is rather the Iron Age which should be put there. The Golden Age of the human race is not behind us but before us; it lies in the perfection of the social order. Our ancestors never saw it; our children will one day arrive there; it is for us to clear the way.

Considerations on the Political
System Now Existing in Europe

by

Friedrich von Gentz

8. Friedrich von Gentz, "Considerations on the Political System Now Existing in Europe," 1818

Friedrich von Gentz (1764–1832), antirevolutionary publicist, took pride in the realism of his political appraisals. As Metternich's most intimate consultant on foreign affairs, he was retained by the rulers of the Danube principality of Wallachia for services that included frequent reports on European politics. The memorandum below is one of these, probably written early in 1818. It provides an introductory sketch of the European political scene as it might be described by an informed and sophisticated observer. To relate the document with others that appear in this section, it may be useful to note the role Gentz assigns to Austro-Prussian cooperation in the European international system, and beyond that, what the ultimate bases of European unity are assumed to be. And you may wish to evaluate Gentz's analysis by checking his predictions against what actually came to pass. [Friedrich von Gentz, *Dépêches inédites du Chevalier de Gentz, aux hospodars de Valachie*, I (Paris, 1876), 354–379. Translation by the editor.]

THE POLITICAL system existing in Europe since 1814 and 1815 is a phenomenon without precedent in the world's history. In place of the principle of equilibrium, or more accurately of counterweights formed by separate alliances, the principle that has governed and too often has also troubled and bloodied Europe for three centuries, there has succeeded a principle of general union, uniting all the states collectively with a federative bond, under the guidance of the five principal Powers, four of which have equal shares in that guidance, while the fifth at this time is still subject to a kind of tutelage, from which it will soon emerge to place itself upon a par with its custodians. The states of the second, third, and fourth rank submit tacitly, though nothing has ever been stipulated in this regard, to the decisions made in common by the preponderant Powers; and so Europe seems really to form a grand political family, united under the auspices of a high tribunal of its own creation, whose members guarantee to themselves and to all parties concerned the peaceful enjoyment of their respective rights.

This scheme of things has its inconveniences. But it is certain that, could it be made durable, it would be after all the best possible combination to assure the prosperity of peoples, and the maintenance of the peace, which is one of its first prerequisites. The strongest objection to the present system is the obvious difficulty of preserving over a long period of time the harmony among the heterogeneous elements that compose it. The most divergent interests, the most conflicting tendencies, and the most contradictory aspirations, views, and secret thoughts are pulled together and for the moment submerged in the common action of a league, which more resembles a coalition created for a particular purpose, than it does a true alliance based on clear and permanent interests. It required unique circumstances to bring such a league into being; it would be contrary to the nature of things and of men for it to replace for long that condition of opposition and conflict which the diversity of positions, interests, and opinions will always impose upon a group of independent Powers, each of which necessarily has its own characteristics and its own system. This perspective is far from unimportant. For one cannot avoid the fact that the collapse of a system now in effect, no matter what new system follows it, will immediately give rise to a state of uncertainty, anxiety, and danger, and will open the way to a new general conflagration with unpredictable results and duration.

Therefore, the most important concern a statesman can have today is the probable duration of this European league, which for the moment has filled the chasm of political dissension but cannot fill it forever, or even for very long. This basically is the only important question of our times; for the peace, the destinies, and the future existence of the peoples of Europe are directly and wholly bound up with it. As long as this kind of general federation exists, questions of the most difficult sort can be worked out smoothly, one way or another, without causing perceptible shocks. But the moment when this system dissolves will be one of the most critical and most terrible that lie before us.

Contemporary opinion is generally doubtful that the present state of affairs can remain stable. It is not believed that an edifice that had its origins in wholly extraordinary events, and which rests upon one single common interest, though that interest be the greatest of all, can survive amid so many surrounding factors for disunity, one or another of which could cause an explosion any day. Even those who possess neither the talents nor the position from which to judge so difficult a question are led by a vague foreboding to regard the Grand Alliance as a meteor always on the verge of extinction; mistrust is part of the spirit of our times. And be it noted besides that the reasons for doubting the stability of the union of sovereigns are much more evident, much easier for the public to grasp, than the less visible reasons for holding the opposite view. But I, having reflected often and deeply on this matter, and possessing all the materials for informed judgment, do not share the conjectures and alarm constantly nourished by many persons. I am persuaded that the European federation—for that is the most accurate term for the present system—is not threatened with immediate ruin. I should not answer for a half-century; but I should not hesitate to answer for ten or even twenty years, a long enough interval I think for everyone to think out the future, and to prepare in time the position that another order of things will require. My opinion is based not on the structure of the system, the extreme fragility of which I myself recognize, but on the situations of the principal Powers that compose it, situations such that no one of these Powers can safely, without risking imminent ruin, leave the circle of its present connections.

The five Powers at the head of the federation are the only ones who could destroy the general system by changing their policies. Squabbles and changes among the others could never have that effect.

Spain and Portugal in one corner, and Sweden and Denmark

in the other, are much too weak and much too far from the center
of Europe for their actions to affect the decisions of the great
Powers.

The Kingdom of the Netherlands is inevitably bound by the
conduct and the relations among its great neighbors; being sus-
pended among France, Britain, and Germany, it can have no
desire but peace, and no principle but to be on good terms with
everybody.

The states of Germany, now that there no longer are and no
longer can be liaisons between themselves and France, are no
more than satellites of the two preponderant bodies; and as long
as Austria and Prussia work together, the other German courts
can only follow their direction.

The states of Italy are squeezed between Austria and France,
and deprived of any will of their own.

The Ottoman Porte would undoubtedly have the power to
make war against Russia, unimpeded by vague ties with the
European federation. But if the Porte should decide some day to
attack Russia without provocation from that Power, the result
probably would be only a separate war that would not disturb
the general system at all. The case would be very different if
Russia were the aggressor; in that case, to which I shall return
later, the present European system would move inevitably toward
catastrophe.

Of the five Powers, which, according to this preliminary de-
scription, are the only ones in position to cause decisive change,
there are three—Austria, Prussia, and Britain—who would regard
such change as total disaster, and would do anything to prevent
it. The other two, France and Russia, *could* have, even in *less*
than ten or twenty years, more or less attractive reasons for leaving their present positions; but they are held there by more important considerations, or by insurmountable hindrances. This I
shall undertake to prove.

Austria, for the past two years, has adopted so pacific a policy
that she must most seriously fear any alteration in the European
system that might tend directly or indirectly to draw her into
new wars. She has reduced her military forces even beyond the
limits and proportions that prudence allows. She has neglected her
army in all respects; and if, as all the signs indicate, she continues
on this false path for several more years, it may be expected that

when summoned one day to take action, she will manage only by painful efforts to reconstitute that army, which is in a process of steady decay. Her finances are recovering little by little; and after two or three years she will be able, in this important respect, to get caught up with her affairs. But that would not make it any easier for her to meet the costs of a serious war. She would have no liquid funds, emergency taxes would not pay for half a campaign, sources of credit are dried up for a long time to come, and nobody, from now on, can count on British subsidies. Therefore, everything combines to bind Austria to a peaceful system. She cannot depart from it without incurring inconveniences and very real dangers, it is pure profit for her to maintain the present state of affairs as long as possible, and, because her central position allows her to play so brilliant a role in the European alliance, she will surely be one of the last to abandon that alliance.

Prussia perhaps would find a few more favorable opportunities than Austria in an overturn of the present system. Still she, too, has important reasons to fear it. Her army is less disorganized than Austria's; and, because she has had the good sense to keep fully organized the militia units that did her such good service in the last war, she would have less difficulty reconstituting an effective army, and it would take her less time. But her provinces are too exhausted to produce an army of over a hundred thousand men, and she is without the means to pay them. Although she is much less burdened with debt than Austria, her finances are by no means flourishing; clear proof of this is that she is now negotiating under very onerous conditions, through English bankers and others, a loan of eighteen million crowns [about fifty million francs], just to cover the deficit of the past two years. Prussia's geographical position has become, despite her recent acquisitions, more difficult and precarious than ever before. Her provinces are vulnerable from all directions. If she strips her western defenses, her Rhine possessions and the whole north of Germany are exposed to French invasion; if she withdraws her forces on the Polish side, she will be in Russia's power. The Prussian government fortunately has recognized that her only safety lies in an intimate combination with Austria, a combination which assures to these two Powers the means of joint disposition over the forces of the rest of Germany. This system has

prevailed over the alternative of a Russian alliance, which has
never had any basis but temporary needs and circumstances. Such
an alliance no longer has a single partisan in Prussia; the King
himself, however attached personally to the Emperor Alexander,
seems to have given it up for good. But the combination with
Austria necessarily implies the maintenance of the general system. For Austria, even while working steadily to cement her
ties with Prussia and to organize the Germanic Confederation in
the interests of the two Powers, still seeks in this only the maintenance of the peace, and considers her association with Prussia
and the whole of Germany (an association which today forms
the basis of her own policy) to be *framed*, so to speak, in the
larger scene of European federation, as the guarantee of general
tranquility; and Prussia will cease to walk the same path as
Austria on the day she thinks of upsetting that system. Thus
Prussia, however one looks at her, is just as interested as Austria
in taking care to avoid anything that might compromise the
peace; and the government at Berlin fears war, and is right to
fear it, as much as and perhaps more than Austria.

England is guided absolutely by the same principles and the
same interests. She has reached her highest point; happy if she
can stay where she is, menaced by incalculable dangers if she
seeks to move out of her position, or if commanding circumstances force her to do so. The debt structure has been pushed to
its extreme limits in England. The best-informed men see no
possibility of extending those limits within ten or fifteen years.
If it is possible within that time to redeem two or three hundred
millions of the public debt, then new loans can be considered;
otherwise any efforts in this direction must necessarily have the
most serious consequences. In the past twenty years England has
grown used to making war on a gigantic scale; each of the recent
years has cost her a hundred million pounds sterling and more.
She cannot accept a secondary role; she must be in the first rank,
or else completely inactive. The British government understands
its position perfectly; it is steeped in it. In the near future it
foresees, not without dread, serious dissensions and perhaps war
with the United States of America, a formidable rival whose
power is growing before our eyes, and whose interests and plans
conflict with those of England in every part of the globe. Thus
many important considerations combine to make the British min-

istry tremble at the very thought of a new war in Europe. She will use every means she has, and even bear heavy sacrifices, to avoid so dangerous a risk. England is the pivot of the European federation; it is she who founded the system, out of her very accurate and very prudent calculation of the great danger to which a new general convulsion would expose her; and also it is she who sustains it, cultivates it, who nurses it always with notable attention, solicitude, and skill. Though she is eternally jealous of France and no less alarmed by the progress of Russia, she carefully avoids giving these two Powers the slightest cause for hostile sentiments. At the same time she treats the German Powers as her true and permanent allies; but even while flooding them with incontestable proofs of her warm confidence, she always reinforces their inclination toward peace, toward avoiding anything that might compromise their good understanding with France and with Russia. This prudent and restrained course is not restricted to the present ministry. It is the necessary outcome of the events that have brought England to the position, brilliant and dangerous at the same time, where she now finds herself; and no matter what ministers govern that country, they will pursue the same policy, perhaps with less skill, aplomb, and dignity than the present ones, but they will always pursue it, at least until a time when the liquidation of a considerable part of the public debt, and of the interest charges and the enormous taxes it carries with it, may permit her to shift to a new course.

I come finally to the two great Powers at the extremities of Europe. These, I admit, do not have the same interest as the others in maintaining the present system. But considering their own situations and their relations with neighboring Powers, there is reason for reassurance regarding the fears they inspire in us.

Let us begin with *France*. Certainly she cannot genuinely enjoy a state of affairs to which she has been forced to submit so as to escape more cruel evils, but which for her has been only a source of humiliation, loss, and bitterness. France will never forget the unprecedented fall that has dropped her from limitless heights of grandeur into nothingness; she will never forget the treaties of 1815, nor the rigor with which fulfillment of those treaties has been demanded, despite the honorable forms devised by the Powers to mask their hard reality. The desire to avenge these insults is in every Frenchman's heart; and though party spirit has smoth-

ered this among some of the noisier ones, of whom there are not
many anyway, sooner or later it will become the dominant sentiment among all elements of the nation. This European federation,
in which so many other Powers have seen and still see their security and their best guarantee, has been nothing but a burden for
France, and can never be an advantage for her. France herself
occupies an important place in it; that is the best thing she can
do for the moment. But she has no need of it for the future.
Her interest is, on the contrary, to dissolve it as soon as possible;
her only chances for recoupment and success lie in divisions
among the great Powers, divisions which would put her in a
position to choose her allies along traditional political lines, and
to recover her strength at the expense of her enemies. These
are all incontestable facts; and the personal character of the King,
the personal characters of his ministers, solemn treaties, special
agreements—all that is of small and transitory weight in such calculations.

It is also true that, Russia excepted, France is the European
Power that has fully recovered its strength most quickly. She has
suffered much, but she has immense resources; and, more important than anything else, her government can command the full
application of her resources better than any other, because her
administrative system far surpasses any other, and because it finds
a perfect instrument for the execution of great projects in a people who are cultivated, intelligent, capable of great things, and
governed now by a free and strong constitution. The existence
of a party that stands, so to speak, outside the constitution and
never ceases to harass and torment the Government is today the
only weak point, the only vulnerable side of France; but in the
eternal nature of things that party must burn itself out in time.
The fiscal wounds will be healed sooner than expected, the army
will be rebuilt within a few years, and the France of 1825 will
no longer resemble the France of 1815 in any way.

But despite all these advantages, France would have great difficulty revising the political system of Europe to suit her tastes,
and until she has accomplished that necessary preliminary, as long
as she is in fact isolated, and a member only of that general association which today takes the place of particular and explicitly
stated alliances, she can undertake nothing substantial. And the
men who direct her affairs are not adventurers who would seize

upon romantic projects. For a very long time to come this Power will be the object of general distrust. The fears and precautions of all Europe will be directed against her for some time yet, and with the slightest hint of an aggressive enterprise, she will revive the league that defeated her in 1814. For a long time yet war against France would be the one popular war in Europe, the only one that would, despite wide hardships, find no lack of supporters, participants, and sacrifice. Governments have learned to compare and balance the dangers that could come upon them from the French side and from the Russian; but the peoples have eyes only for France. The hatreds and fears that France has inspired everywhere will not be quieted so soon.

The French government is too intelligent and too perceptive not to judge and appreciate this state of affairs. First of all, it needs a number of years to recover from its wounds. Five or six years will be absolutely necessary for this. At the end of this time, even if one supposes the French government really determined to recover a major role in the affairs of Europe, it will have to find a way to detach itself from the Grand Alliance, and to substitute for it relations based on common interests with one or the other principal Power—conditions that will not be easy to fulfill. Without achieving this first, France can undertake nothing, or certainly will fail in her undertakings. As long as the league survives among the other Powers, France, even supposing full recovery of her strength, must confine herself to speculations about the future. This reasoning, in which I have left out of account the shocks that the death of the King or other internal events might cause, confirms me in the opinion that it will not be France that overturns the present system; but I am persuaded at the same time that she will profit from the destruction of the system, when other circumstances cause it to fall.

I enter upon the ticklish subject of *Russia* with far less assurance. There, where the absolute will of a single man decides everything and where, to add to the difficulty, the character of that man is problematical, judgments and conjectures find no solid foundations, and permit no better than guesswork. Be that as it may, it is well worth the trouble frankly to declare the pros and cons on a matter so important, without claiming too strong a probability for one side or the other.

The Emperor Alexander, despite all the zeal and enthusiasm he has consistently shown for the Grand Alliance, is the sovereign who could most easily get along without it. He needs nobody's support; if his position be threatened, at least it cannot be threatened from outside his Empire, for all Europe fears his power and has reason to fear it. For him the Grand Alliance is only an implement with which he exercises in general affairs the influence that is one of the main objects of his ambition. It is a comfortable and tractable implement, which he makes use of with great skill, but which he will destroy on the first day he thinks he can replace it with something more direct and more effective. His interest in the preservation of the system is not, as is true of Austria, Prussia, or England, an interest based on necessity or fear; it is a free and calculated interest, which he is in a position to renounce as soon as a different system should offer him greater advantages.

The Emperor of Russia is, moreover, the one sovereign fully in a position to undertake major enterprises at any time. He is at the head of the one standing army really capable of action in Europe today. Nothing could resist the first assault of that army. It is unnecessary to repeat here what we have long known about the geographical situation of Russia and that of her neighbors. None of the obstacles that restrain and thwart the other sovereigns—divided authority, constitutional forms, public opinion, etc.—exists for the Emperor of Russia. What he dreams of at night he can carry out in the morning.

Surely, it takes very considerable counterarguments to give reassurance against dangers as evident as these. But let us see the reverse of the coin.

First, one would have to know whether the Emperor Alexander has the will or desire to bring about changes, and overturn the present system. People say the man is impenetrable, and therefore everybody feels free to judge his intentions. I do not wish to fall into the same error; but I have considered the question long enough to know how difficult it is to resolve it. I know all there is to be said about his consuming energy, his ambition, his dissimulation. But I also know of qualities in him of quite another stamp. His chivalrous loyalty would never permit him an act of betrayal. He sets great store by the good opinion of men, perhaps even more than he does by glory as such. The titles of

Peacemaker, Protector of the Weak, or Regenerator of the Empire have more charm for him than Conqueror. Religious sentiments, which are *not* hypocritical, have for many years so predominated in his mind that all is subordinated to them. A prince in whom good and bad are mixed in so singular a manner must necessarily be the object of many doubts, and it would be rash to say what his conduct would be in this or that possible situation. But when I think of him placed in definite given circumstances, it seems to me less rash to judge what he would do and what he would not do in response to those circumstances. He considers himself the founder, the creator of the European federation; he would like to be considered its chief. For two years he has not dictated a memorandum or a diplomatic document without extolling this system as the century's glory, and as the salvation of the world. Is it probable, is it possible that in the face of all these testimonials, which fill the archives of governments, which are the substance of a hundred proclamations, in the face of a public opinion that respects and fears him, and of a religion he honors, he should embark upon unjust and pointless enterprises, to destroy a work from which he expects his immortality? I cannot easily believe in a revolution that abrupt. Though many people say that all that is a game and a comedy, I have a right to ask for proof. Why should he not be devoted to this system by principle and by preference? Why should he not prefer this kind of glory, which, moreover, fits very well with a secret thought of peaceful supremacy, to the risks of wars and turmoil, whose outcome must always seem doubtful to one who cannot, like Napoleon, hope to make the outcome certain by virtue of military talents of the first order?

Let us suppose all the same that there should occur such an abrupt change in the ideas and sentiments the Emperor has so far expressed that he should decide to defy public opinion, the scruples of conscience, the most solemn testimony, and the most sacred engagements. We then come to another question. Would he have the means to accomplish projects of aggrandizement and domination, on a base so uncertain and so impermanent?

Financial distress, the common malady of all European governments, lies heavy upon the Russian as well; and emergency funds, in the quantity needed for extended campaigns, would be sought in vain, inside or outside the Empire. You could reply

to this that the Russian armies, pushed beyond the frontiers by
vigorous and swift operations, would no longer cost the country
anything, and would find enough to live on. But this argument
forgets that the requisition system, easy to apply in a passing
invasion, does not suit a war or an occupation of long duration,
and that the abuse the French made of this system made them
an object of hatred among the peoples, and that a conqueror
obliged to base his plan of operations on requisitions would
immediately become generally odious, and would find within a
year the same fate Napoleon had after fifteen years of unprecedented victories.

As long as Austria and Prussia hold together, Russia will not
be able to undertake limited and isolated campaigns. To attain
any end comparable to the vast projects attributed to her, she
would have to move on an immense front, from the Memel to
the Carpathians. Five hundred thousand men would not be too
many for such an undertaking. At the beginning she would find
little resistance; for, as I observed before, defenses would not be
good. But little by little the opposing forces would form; all
Germany, more attached to her independence than ever, would
be aroused, and would provide Austria and Prussia with the
help needed for swift re-establishment of the equilibrium. Without counting the cooperation of England—cooperation more formidable for Russia than a land army of two hundred thousand
men—the Russian armies, after a few brilliant and sterile successes,
would find themselves everywhere repulsed, and the Emperor
Alexander, having lost all the fruits of his former policy, would
reap from the one he had embraced only regrets, embarrassments,
and dangers from which he could not extricate himself for the
rest of his life.

The one single expedition Russia could undertake without directly encountering these enormous difficulties would be the one
said to have threatened the Porte for a long time. It is certain
that, given the present condition of the other Powers, Russian
armies could have crossed the Danube and been in full march
against Constantinople without bringing on the slightest hostile
movement at their rear or on their flanks. But such successes,
even supposing them much easier than they are in reality, would
be no less ephemeral and illusory. For if Austria, Prussia, and
England stay in agreement—France counting for nothing in this

calculation—the Powers can never allow the Porte's territory to be invaded or dismembered by the Russians. Their opposition might be slow, but it need only be sure, to keep the Emperor from exposing himself to a reaction whose consequences might be quite as disastrous for him as those of a vain effort against Germany. It is this consideration that makes me persist in the belief that the present system, even though the Porte is not included in it, is one of the strongest guarantees of its security and its rights, and in the belief that the Holy Alliance, which seems to be regarded with an evil eye in Constantinople, and which is after all only a fanciful ornamentation on the real federation, is one of the Porte's greatest assets.

We see then that in the last analysis the position of Russia, despite the immensity of resources, is infinitely more like that of France than might have been supposed. Just like France, Russia cannot undertake anything without having *previously* changed the European system, by detaching one or another of its essential members and making it her permanent ally. Only then could she break out of line and try her strength, be it against Germany or the Porte. If Prussia had stayed with Russia in the situation of 1814 [cooperation against Austria], it would today be up to the Emperor Alexander to choose among the roles of protector, of dictator, or of tyrant over Europe. This danger is past; and though the government at Vienna has made some mistakes, it has fully expiated them by the active part it took in Prussia's healthy repentance. In whatever hands the direction of that Power's affairs may fall, she will not soon return to her old erroneous ways. Russia can no longer hope to interest England in any project whatever that is contrary to the general interest. All that remains to her, then, as a last resort and a last bugbear, is a separate alliance with France. Such an alliance is possible; it is even one of the least unlikely and the most frightening possibilities of the future. But it needs time and much time for it to ripen. And as the two Powers have no point of contact whatever, the intervening States and England would be guilty of negligence or weakness difficult to imagine, should they let themselves be taken unawares by so fatal a combination.

These reflections lead to a conclusion as remarkable as it is reassuring. What at first glance seems the weakest part of the present system is precisely what gives it force. France and Russia are today the only two Powers who could threaten Europe with a new upheaval, and they are rendered incapable of harm as long as the *middle line*, formed by Powers whose only interest and whose only desire is peace, is not broken. Austria, Prussia, and England, each little disposed today and little prepared for a serious war, comparatively and individually impotent, peaceful by necessity, but still strong enough for joint resistance, are the true rampart of the common security of Europe; and the colossi that occupy the two extremities, breaking against this central dike for as long as it lasts, must for a long time to come seek their advantage and their glory in preserving an order of things that they cannot hope to destroy.

Add to these considerations the general situation of the peoples, their horror of war, the attention that must be paid to them, the penury of all the governments, the evident inclinations of the cabinets at London, Vienna, and Berlin, and what the soundest data and the most reasonable calculations tell us of the reigning principles in France and in Russia—I think that very great probabilities join in pointing to the maintenance of the general peace, and of the political system, which, with all its imperfections and all its faults, is today its foundation and its guarantee.

9. Intervention in Germany: Teplitz and Carlsbad, 1819

The Vienna Act of 1815 setting up the German Confederation had included, as a sop to German liberal sentiments, which the authors did not yet dare fully to antagonize, a provision (Article 13) that the several German states would establish representative constitutions. The governments of some of the smaller states in the South, seeking popularity with their subjects and political independence from their greater neighbors, did provide constitutions and elected assemblies. Metternich's anxiety at what might develop from this trend led to his meeting with the Prussian king and government at Teplitz in the summer of 1819, soon after the Kotzebue murder. The policies agreed upon there by Austria and Prussia are the political essentials of the Carlsbad Decrees, adopted by the Diet of the Confederation in September, establishing close controls over universities and the press. [Metternich to the Emperor Francis: Metternich, *Memoirs*, III (1881), 299–308; the Teplitz Convention: Heinrich von Treitschke, *History of Germany in the Nineteenth Century*, trans. Eden and Cedar Paul, III (London, 1917), 628–631.]

World Peace Foundation
Pamphlet Series

THE UNITED STATES OF EUROPE

BY

VICTOR HUGO

PUBLISHED BIMONTHLY BY THE

WORLD PEACE FOUNDATION
40 MT. VERNON STREET, BOSTON

October, 1914
Vol. IV. No. 6. Part II

THE UNITED STATES OF EUROPE

PRESIDENTIAL ADDRESS AT THE INTERNATIONAL PEACE CONGRESS, PARIS, AUGUST 22, 1849

By Victor Hugo

Gentlemen:—Many of you have come from the most distant points of the globe, your hearts full of holy and religious feelings. You count in your ranks men of letters, philosophers, ministers of the Christian religion, writers of eminence, and public men justly popular for their talents. You, gentlemen, have wished to adopt Paris as the center of this meeting, whose sympathies, full of gravity and conviction, do not merely apply to one nation, but to the whole world. You come to add another principle of a still superior—of a more august kind—to those that now direct statesmen, rulers, and legislators. You turn over, as it were, the last page of the Gospel—that page which imposes peace on the children of the same God; and in this capital, which has as yet only decreed fraternity among citizens, you are about to proclaim the brotherhood of mankind.

Gentlemen, we bid you a hearty welcome! In the presence of such a thought and such an act, there can be no room for the expression of personal thanks. Permit me, then, in the first words which I pronounce in your hearing, to raise my thoughts higher than myself, and, as it were, to omit all mention of the great honor which you have just conferred upon me, in order that I may think of nothing else than the great thing which we have met to do.

Gentlemen, this sacred idea, universal peace, all nations bound together in a common bond, the Gospel for their supreme law, mediation substituted for war—this holy sentiment, I ask you, is it practicable? Can it be realized? Many practical men, many public men grown old in the management of affairs, answer in the negative. But I answer with you, and I answer without hesitation, Yes! and I shall shortly try to prove it to you. I go still further. I do not merely say it is capable of being put into practice, but I add that it is inevitable, and that its execution is only a question of time, and may be hastened or retarded. The law which rules the world is not, cannot be different from the law of God. But the divine law is not

one of war—it is peace.   Men commenced by conflict, as the creation
did by chaos.   Whence are they coming?   From wars—that is
evident.   But whither are they going?   To peace—that is equally
evident.   When you enunciate those sublime truths, it is not to be
wondered at that your assertion should be met by a negative; it is
easy to understand that your faith will be encountered by incredulity;
it is evident that in this period of trouble and of dissension the idea
of universal peace must surprise and shock, almost like the apparition
of something impossible and ideal; it is quite clear that all will
call it utopian; but for me, who am but an obscure laborer in this
great work of the nineteenth century, I accept this opposition without
being astonished or discouraged by it.   Is it possible that you can
do otherwise than turn aside your head and shut your eyes, as if in
bewilderment, when in the midst of the darkness which still envelopes
you, you suddenly open the door that lets in the light of the future?

Gentlemen, if four centuries ago, at the period when war was
made by one district against the other, between cities, and between
provinces—if, I say, some one had dared to predict to Lorraine, to
Picardy, to Normandy, to Brittany, to Auvergne, to Provence,
to Dauphiny, to Burgundy,—"A day shall come when you will no
longer make wars—a day shall come when you will no longer arm men
one against the other—a day shall come when it will no longer be
said that the Normans are attacking the Picards, or that the people
of Lorraine are repulsing the Burgundians:—you will still have many
disputes to settle, interests to contend for, difficulties to resolve;
but do you know what you will substitute instead of armed men,
instead of cavalry and infantry, of cannon, of falconets, lances,
pikes and swords:—you will select, instead of all this destructive
array, a small box of wood, which you will term a ballot-box, and
from which shall issue—what?—an assembly—an assembly in which
you shall all live—an assembly which shall be, as it were, the soul
of all—a supreme and popular council, which shall decide, judge,
resolve everything—which shall make the sword fall from every
hand, and excite the love of justice in every heart—which shall say to
each, 'Here terminates your right, there commences your duty:
lay down your arms!   Live in peace!'   And in that day you will
all have one common thought, common interests, a common destiny;
you will embrace each other, and recognize each other as children
of the same blood, and of the same race;   that day you will no
longer be hostile tribes,—you will be a people;   you will no longer be

Burgundy, Normandy, Brittany, or Provence,—you will be France! You will no longer make appeals to war—you will do so to civilization." If, at the period I speak of, some one had uttered these words, all men of a serious and positive character, all prudent and cautious men, all the great politicians of the period, would have cried out, "What a dreamer! what a fantastic dream! How little this pretended prophet is acquainted with the human heart! What ridiculous folly! what an absurd chimera!" Yet, gentlemen, time has gone on and on, and we find that this dream, this folly, this absurdity, has been realized! And I insist upon this, that the man who would have dared to utter so sublime a prophecy would have been pronounced a madman for having dared to pry into the designs of the Deity. Well, then, you at this moment say—and I say it with you—we who are assembled here, say to France, to England, to Prussia, to Austria, to Spain, to Italy, to Russia—we say to them, "A day will come when from your hands also the arms you have grasped will fall. A day will come when war will appear as absurd, and be as impossible, between Paris and London, between St. Petersburg and Berlin, between Vienna and Turin, as it would be now between Rouen and Amiens, between Boston and Philadelphia. A day will come when you, France—you, Russia—you, Italy— you, England—you, Germany—all of you, nations of the Continent, will, without losing your distinctive qualities and your glorious individuality, be blended into a superior unity, and constitute a European fraternity, just as Normandy, Brittany, Burgundy, Lorraine, Alsace,[1] have been blended into France. A day will come when the only battle-field will be the market open to commerce and the mind opening to new ideas. A day will come when bullets and bombshells will be replaced by votes, by the universal suffrage of nations, by the venerable arbitration of a great Sovereign Senate, which will be to Europe what the Parliament is to England, what the Diet is to Germany, what the Legislative Assembly is to France. A day will come when a cannon will be exhibited in public museums, just as an instrument of torture is now, and people will be astonished how such a thing could have been. A day will come when those two immense groups, the United States of America and the United States of Europe, shall be seen placed in presence of each other, extending the hand of fellowship across the ocean, exchanging their

[1] The address was written twenty-two years before Alsace and Lorraine became a German crown land by the Treaty of Frankfort.

produce, their commerce, their industry, their arts, their genius, clearing the earth, peopling the deserts, improving creation under the eye of the Creator, and uniting, for the good of all, these two irresistible and infinite powers, the fraternity of men and the power of God." Nor is it necessary that four hundred years should pass away for that day to come. We live in a rapid period, in the most impetuous current of events and ideas which has ever borne away humanity; and at the period in which we live, a year suffices to do the work of a century.

But, French, English, Germans, Russians, Slavs, Europeans, Americans, what have we to do in order to hasten the advent of that great day? We must love each other! To love each other is, in this immense labor of pacification, the best manner of aiding God! God desires that this sublime object should be accomplished. And to arrive at it you are yourselves witnesses of what the Deity is doing on all sides. See what discoveries are every day issuing from human genius—discoveries which all tend to the same object —Peace! What immense progress! What simplification! How Nature is allowing herself to be more and more subjugated by man! How matter every day becomes still more the handmaid of intellect, and the auxiliary of civilization! How the causes of war vanish with the causes of suffering! How people far separated from each other so lately, now almost touch! How distances become less and less; and this rapid approach, what is it but the commencement of fraternity? Thanks to railroads, Europe will soon be no larger than France was in the middle ages. Thanks to steamships, we now traverse the mighty ocean more easily than the Mediterranean was formerly crossed. Before long, men will traverse the earth, as the gods of Homer did the sky, in three paces! But yet a little time, and the electric wire of concord shall encircle the globe and embrace the world. And here, gentlemen, when I contemplate this vast amount of efforts and of events, all of them marked by the finger of God—when I regard this sublime object, the well-being of mankind—peace,—when I reflect on all that Providence has done in favor of it, and human policy against it, a sad and bitter thought presents itself to my mind. It results, from a comparison of statistical accounts, that the nations of Europe expend each year for the maintenance of armies a sum amounting to two thousand millions of francs, and which, by adding the expense of maintaining establishments of war, amounts to three thousand millions. Add to this the lost produce of the days of work of more than 2,000,000 men—the healthiest, the most vigorous, the youngest, the élite of our population —a produce which you will not estimate at less than one thousand millions, and you will be convinced that the standing armies of Europe cost annually more than four thousand millions.

Gentlemen, peace has now lasted thirty-two years, and yet in thirty-two years the enormous sum of 128,000,000 has been expended during a time of peace on account of war![2] Suppose that the people of Europe, in place of mistrusting each other, entertaining jealousy of each other, hating each other, had become fast friends—suppose they had said, that before they were French, or English, or German, they were men, and that if nations form countries, the human race forms a family; and that enormous sum of 128,000,000, so madly and so vainly spent in consequence of such mistrust, let it be spent in acts of mutual confidence— these 128,000,000 that have been lavished on hatred, let them be bestowed on love—let them be given to peace, instead of war—give them to labor, to intelligence, to industry, to commerce, to navigation, to agriculture, to science, to art; and then draw your conclusions. If for the last thirty-two years this enormous sum had been expended in this manner, America in the meantime aiding Europe, know you what would have happened? The face of the world would have been changed. Isthmuses would be cut through, channels formed for rivers, tunnels bored through mountains. Railroads would cover the two continents; the merchant navy of the globe would have increased a hundred-fold. There would be nowhere barren plains, nor moors, nor marshes. Cities would be found where there are now only deserts. Ports would be sunk where there are now only rocks. Asia would be rescued to civilization; Africa would be rescued to man; abundance would gush forth on every side, from every vein of the earth, at the touch of man, like the living stream from the rock beneath the rod of Moses. Misery would be no longer found; and with misery, what do you think would disappear? Revolutions. Yes, the face of the world would be changed! In place of mutually destroying each other, men would pacifically extend themselves over the earth. In place of conspiring for revolution, men would combine to establish colonies! In place of introducing barbarism into civilization, civilization would replace barbarism.

[2] Victor Hugo was speaking in 1849. His reference was undoubtedly to France. The world's armament bill for the year 1845 was about $560,000,000. To-day it is nearly five times that. See table in this pamphlet giving statistics for 1912–13.

You see, gentlemen, in what a state of blindness war has placed nations and rulers. If the 128,000,000 given for the last thirty-two years by Europe to the war which was not waged had been given to the peace which existed, we positively declare that nothing of what is now passing in Europe would have occurred. The Continent in place of being a battle-field would have become a universal workshop, and in place of this sad and terrible spectacle of Piedmont prostrated, of the Eternal City given up to the miserable oscillations of human policy, of Venice and noble Hungary struggling heroically, France uneasy, impoverished, and gloomy; misery, mourning, civil war, gloom in the future—in place, I say, of so sad a spectacle, we should have before our eyes hope, joy, benevolence, the efforts of all toward the common good, and we should everywhere behold the majestic ray of universal concord issue forth from civilization. And this fact is worthy of meditation—that revolutions have been owing to those very precautions against war. All has been done—all this expenditure has been incurred, against an imaginary danger. Misery, which was the only real danger, has by these very means been augmented. We have been fortifying ourselves against a chimerical peril; our eyes have been turned to all sides except to the one where the black spot was visible. We have been looking out for wars when there were none, and we have not seen the revolutions that were coming on. Yet, gentlemen, let us not despair. Let us, on the contrary, hope more enthusiastically than ever. Let us not allow ourselves to be daunted by momentary commotions—convulsions which, peradventure, are necessary for so mighty a production. Let us not be unjust to the time in which we live—let us not look upon it otherwise than as it is. It is a prodigious and admirable epoch after all; and the 19th century will be, I do not hesitate to say, the greatest in the page of history. As I stated a few minutes since, all kinds of progress are being revealed and manifested almost simultaneously, the one producing the other—the cessation of international animosities, the effacing of frontiers on the maps, and of prejudices from the heart—the tendency toward unity, the softening of manners, the advancement of education, the diminution of penalties, the domination of the most literary languages—all are at work at the same time—political economy, science, industry, philosophy, legislation; and all tend to the same object—the creation of happiness and of good will, that is to say—and for my own part, it is the object to which I shall always direct myself—the extinction of

misery at home, and the extinction of war abroad. Yes, the period
of revolutions is drawing to a close—the era of improvements is
beginning. The education of people is no longer of the violent kind;
it is now assuming a peaceful nature. The time has come when
Providence is about to substitute for the disorderly action of the
agitator the religious and quiet energy of the peacemaker. Hence-
forth the object of all great and true policy will be this—to cause all
nationalities to be recognized, to restore the historic unity of nations,
and enlist this unity in the cause of civilization by means of peace—
to enlarge the sphere of civilization, to set a good example to people
who are still in a state of barbarism—to substitute the system of
arbitration for that of battles—and, in a word—and all is comprised
in this—to make justice pronounce the last word that the old world
used to pronounce by force.

Gentlemen, I say in conclusion, and let us be encouraged by this
thought, mankind has not entered on this providential course to-day
for the first time. In our ancient Europe, England took the first
step, and by her example declared to the people "You are free!"
France took the second step, and announced to the people "You
are sovereigns!" Let us now take the third step, and all simultaneously, France, England, Germany, Italy, Europe, America—
let us proclaim to all nations "You are brethren!"

THE MAP OF EUROPE

BY JOSEPH MAZZINI

Bad governments have disfigured the design of God, which you
may see clearly marked out, as far, at least, as regards Europe, by the
courses of the great rivers, by the lines of the lofty mountains, and
by other geographical conditions; they have disfigured it by conquest,
by greed, by jealousy of the just sovereignty of others; disfigured it
so much that to-day there is perhaps no nation, except England and
France, whose confines correspond to this design. They did not, and
they do not, recognize any country except their own families and
dynasties, the egoism of caste. But the divine design will infallibly
be fulfilled. Natural divisions, the innate spontaneous tendencies
of the peoples, will replace the arbitrary divisions sanctioned by bad
governments.

The map of Europe will be remade. The Countries of the People will rise, defined by the voice of the free, upon the ruins of the Countries of Kings and privileged castes. Between these countries there will be harmony and brotherhood. And then the work of Humanity for the general amelioration, for the discovery and application of the real law of life, carried on in association and distributed according to local capacities, will be accomplished by peaceful and progressive development.

The cause of peace is not the cause of cowardice. If peace is sought to be defended or preserved for the safety of the luxurious and the timid, it is a sham, and the peace will be base. War is better, and the peace will be broken. If peace is to be maintained, it must be by brave men, who have come up to the same height as the hero, namely, the will to carry their life in their hand, and stake it at any instant for their principle, but who have gone one step beyond the hero, and will not seek another man's life; men who have, by their intellectual insight, or else by their moral elevation, attained such a perception of their own intrinsic worth, that they do not think property or their own body a sufficient good to be saved by such dereliction of principle as treating a man like a sheep. If the rising generation can be provoked to think it unworthy to nestle into every abomination of the past, and shall feel the generous darings of austerity and virtue, then war has a short day. Whenever we see the doctrine of peace embraced by a nation, we may be assured it will not be one that invites injury; but one, on the contrary, which has a friend in the bottom of the heart of every man, even of the violent and the base; one against which no weapon can prosper; one which is looked upon as the asylum of the human race and has the blessings of mankind. . . . In this broad America of God and man, where the forest is only now falling, and the green earth opens to the inundation of emigrant men from all quarters of oppression and guilt,—here, where not a family, not a few men, but mankind, shall say what shall be,—here, we ask, Shall it be War, or shall it be Peace?—*From Emerson's Essay on War.*

> Were half the power that fills the world with terror,
>   Were half the wealth bestowed on camps and courts,
> Given to redeem the human mind from error,
>   There were no need of arsenals or forts.—*Longfellow.*

THE WORLD'S ANNUAL ARMAMENT BILL
IN TIME OF PEACE

From "The Drain of Armaments."

Country	Fiscal Year	Expended for Army	Expended for Navy	Total Military Charge
GREAT BRITAIN AND THE CONTINENT OF EUROPE				
Austria-Hungary .	1913	[1] $115,381,000	$15,176,000	$130,557,000
Belgium	1912	13,119,000		13,119,000
[2] Bulgaria	1912	7,817,000		7,817,000
Denmark	1912–13	5,337,000	3,013,000	8,350,000
France	1912	[1] 177,656,000	81,693,000	259,349,000
Germany	1912–13	201,003,000	111,964,000	312,967,000
Great Britain . . .	1911–12	134,850,000	216,194,000	351,044,000
[2] Greece	1912	4,155,000	1,699,000	5,854,000
Italy	1912–13	[1] 83,284,000	41,859,000	125,143,000
Netherlands . . .	1913	13,412,000	8,092,000	21,504,000
Norway	1911–12	4,063,000	1,539,000	5,602,000
Portugal	1910–11	9,279,000	4,317,000	13,596,000
Rumania	1912–13	14,365,000		14,365,000
Russia	1912	289,911,000	81,960,000	371,871,000
[2] Servia	1912	5,699,000		5,699,000
Spain	1912	[1] 36,353,000	13,546,000	49,899,000
Sweden	1913	14,884,000	7,032,000	21,916,000
Switzerland . . ,	1912	8,516,000		8,516,000
Turkey	1912–13	39,374,000	5,614,000	44,988,000
Total (Great Britain) and the Continent)		$1,178,458,000	$593,698,000	$1,772,156,000
UNITED STATES . .	1911–12	[3] $107,787,000	$136,390,000	$244,177,000
JAPAN	1912–13	47,066,000	46,510,000	93,576,000
BRITISH INDIA . . .	1911–12	101,409,000		101,409,000
MEXICO AND SOUTH AMERICA				
Argentina	1912	$12,232,000	$11,856,000	$24,088,000
Brazil	1912	25,425,000	14,969,000	40,394,000
Chile	1912	12,164,000	11,416,000	23,580,000
Colombia	1913			2,661,000
Ecuador	1910			2,031,000
Mexico	1912–13	Army and Navy		10,790,000
Peru	1911	not differentiated		2,425,000
Uruguay	1910–11			4,946,000
Venezuela	1912–13			1,834,000
Total (Mexico and South America) .				$112,749,000
WORLD TOTAL				$2,324,067,000

[1] Including Austrian Landwehr and Hungarian Honved (Honved -1912), French Gendarmes, Italian Carabinieri, Spanish Guarda Civil and Carabineros.
[2] These expenditures are the normal peace expenditures only. The cost of the Balkan War was met by special appropriations.
[3] This excludes civil expenditures charged to War Department ($43,262,000). United States Treasurer's statement shows a total of $151,049,000.

INTERNATIONAL LIBRARY
Edited by EDWIN D. MEAD
PUBLISHED BY THE WORLD PEACE FOUNDATION
CLOTH BOUND

ADDRESSES ON WAR. By CHARLES SUMNER. 8vo, xxvii+321 pages.
Postpaid $0.60

AMERICAN ADDRESSES AT THE SECOND HAGUE CONFERENCE.
Edited by JAMES BROWN SCOTT. 8vo, xlviii+217 pages. Postpaid . . . 1.65

DISCOURSES ON WAR. By WILLIAM ELLERY CHANNING. 8vo, lxi+229
pages. Postpaid 60

ETERNAL PEACE AND OTHER INTERNATIONAL ESSAYS. By
IMMANUEL KANT. 8vo, xxiv+179 pages 75

ETHICS OF FORCE. By H. E. WARNER. 8vo, v+126 pages. Postpaid, .55

FIRST BOOK OF WORLD LAW. By RAYMOND L. BRIDGMAN. 8vo,
v+308 pages. Postpaid 1.65

FIRST HAGUE CONFERENCE. By ANDREW D. WHITE. 8vo, vi+125
pages. Postpaid 55

FISHERIES ARBITRATION ARGUMENT OF ELIHU ROOT. Edited,
with Introduction and Appendix, by JAMES BROWN SCOTT. 8vo, cli+523
pages. Postpaid 3.50

FUTURE OF WAR. By JEAN DE BLOCH. 8vo, lxxix+380 pages. Postpaid, .65

GREAT DESIGN OF HENRY IV. With Introduction by EDWIN D. MEAD.
8vo, xxi+91 pages. Postpaid 55

INTERNATIONAL ARBITRAL LAW AND PROCEDURE. By JACKSON H.
RALSTON. 8vo, xix+352 pages. Postpaid 2.20

INTER-RACIAL PROBLEMS. Papers communicated to the First Universal
Races Congress, London, July 26-29, 1911. Edited by G. SPILLER.
Quarto, xvi+485 pages. Postpaid 2.40

MOHONK ADDRESSES. By EDWARD EVERETT HALE and DAVID J. BREWER.
8vo, xxviii+150 pages. Postpaid 1.00

MORAL DAMAGE OF WAR. By WALTER WALSH. 8vo, xiii+462 pages.
Postpaid 90

NEW PEACE MOVEMENT. By WILLIAM I. HULL. 8vo, xi+217 pages.
Postpaid 1.00

PRIZE ORATIONS OF THE INTERCOLLEGIATE PEACE ASSOCIATION.
Edited, with introduction by STEPHEN F. WESTON. 8vo, xiii+185 pages.
Postpaid 75

PUBLIC INTERNATIONAL UNIONS. By PAUL S. REINSCH. 8vo, viii+
189 pages. Postpaid 1.65

SIR RANDAL CREMER. By HOWARD EVANS. 8vo, 356 pages. Postpaid, 1.40

TEXTS OF THE PEACE CONFERENCES AT THE HAGUE, 1899 and 1907.
Edited by JAMES BROWN SCOTT. 8vo, xxxiv+447 pages. Postpaid . . 2.20

TWO HAGUE CONFERENCES. By WILLIAM I. HULL. 8vo, xiv+516
pages. Postpaid 1.65

WAR INCONSISTENT WITH THE RELIGION OF JESUS CHRIST. By
DAVID LOW DODGE. 8vo, xxiv+168 pages. Postpaid 60

WORLD ORGANIZATION. By RAYMOND L. BRIDGMAN. 8vo, vi+172
pages. Postpaid 60

PAPER BOUND

BETHINK YOURSELVES! By LEO TOLSTOI. 6½ x 4½ in., 50 pages. Postpaid . $0.10

BLOOD OF THE NATION. By DAVID STARR JORDAN. 6¾ x 4¾ in., 82 pages.
Postpaid 15

DUEL BETWEEN FRANCE AND GERMANY. By CHARLES SUMNER. 7½ x 5¼
in., 76 pages. Postpaid 20

KING'S EASTER. By HARRIET PRESCOTT SPOFFORD. 7½ x 5 in., 16 pages. Postpaid . .10

LEAGUE OF PEACE, A. By ANDREW CARNEGIE. 6½ x 4½ in., 47 pages. Postpaid, .10

OUTLINE OF LESSONS ON WAR AND PEACE. By LUCIA AMES MEAD.
8 x 5½ in., 28 pages. Postpaid 10

PATRIOTISM AND THE NEW INTERNATIONALISM. By LUCIA AMES MEAD.
6¾ x 4¾ in., 125 pages. Postpaid 20

SYLLABUS OF LECTURES ON INTERNATIONAL CONCILIATION. By DAVID
STARR JORDAN and EDWARD B. KREHBIEL. 9¼ x 5¾ in., 180 pages. Postpaid . .75

TRUE GRANDEUR OF NATIONS. By CHARLES SUMNER. 7½ x 5¼ in., 132
pages. Postpaid 20

WAR SYSTEM OF THE COMMONWEALTH OF NATIONS. By CHARLES SUMNER.
7½ x 5¼ in., 107 pages. Postpaid 20

WHAT SHALL WE SAY? By DAVID STARR JORDAN. 9¼ x 6 in., 82 pages. Postpaid, .35

Europe: Its Condition and Prospects

by

Giuseppe Mazzini

Art. III.—Europe : its Condition and Prospects.

Correspondence respecting the Foreign Refugees in London.
Presented to both Houses of Parliament by command of
Her Majesty, 1852.

THE literature of the Continent during the last few years has
been essentially political, revolutionary, and warlike. Out of
ten historical works, seven at least speak to us, from a favourable
point of view or otherwise, of a revolution now extinct; out of
ten polemical, political, economical, or other works, seven at
least proclaim or combat a revolution about to take place. The
first bear the impress of terror, the last are full of gigantic hopes,
though most imperfectly defined. Calm has fled from the minds
of writers. Poetry is silent, as if frightened by the storm now
gathering in the hearts of men. Romance becomes rarer every
day; it would find no readers. Pure art is a myth. Style itself
is changed; when it is not commonplace, when it retains something of that individual originality which every style ought to

have, it is sharp, cutting, biting. The pen seems, as it were, sword-shaped; all the world thinks and writes as if it felt itself on the eve of a battle.

From the midst of this tempest which we point out, because to sleep is to perish amid the storm, voices are heard exclaiming, "Beware! Society is in danger. Anarchy threatens us. The barbarians are at our gates. Revolutions destroy all the guarantees of order; from change to change we are plunging into nothingness. We have conceded too much; we must retrace our steps and strengthen power at all price." Other voices reply to them,—" It is too late, your society is dead, corrupted; hasten to bury it. The salvation of the world is in us, in an entirely new order of things, in a society founded upon a basis diametrically opposed to yours." Flags cross each other in the air in infinite variety. *Liberty, Authority, Nationality,* 1815, *Labour, Property, Rights, Duties, Association, Individualism* —all devices are seen. It is the night of the Brocksberg—a sort of intellectual and moral chaos, to which scarcely anything analogous is to be found, unless we go back some eighteen centuries in the history of the world, to the fall of the Roman Empire, when the ancient gods were dying; when the human mind was wavering between the sceptical epicurism of the masters and the aspiration of the slaves to the UNKNOWN GOD; when the earth trembled under the steps of unknown races, impelled by a mysterious, irresistible power towards the centre of European society.

What is the signification of this prolonged and still ascending crisis, notwithstanding all the efforts which are made to over come it? Have they, these *barbarians* of our days, a Rome in which great destinies are to be accomplished, and towards which, like Attila and his hordes, they are impelled by an invisible hand; or do they march onward to lose themselves in deserts, without object, without a tomb, without a useful memorable trace in history? Are we advancing towards anarchy or towards a new mode of things,—towards dissolution or towards a transformed life? All ask themselves this question; all could resolve it, if the point of view of each man were not narrowed by his position in some one of the adverse camps, by the now prevailing habit of judging of the depth, the intensity, and the direction of the European current by the passing ebullitions of the surface, and by a prejudice, presently to be defined, which for half a century has influenced almost all appreciations of the political situation.

And yet this question *must* be resolved. It is a vital one. It necessarily contains a rule for our actions. A law of Solon decreed that degradation should attach itself to those who in an insurrection abstained from taking part on one side or the other.

It was a just and holy law, founded on the belief, then instinctive
in the heart of Solon, but now comprehended and expressed in a
thousand formulas, in the solidarity of humanity. It is so now
more than ever. What! you are in the midst of an up-rising,
not of a town, but of the whole human race; you have brute
force on the one side, and right on the other; you march between
proscription and martyrdom, between the scaffold and the altar;
whole nations are struggling under oppression; generations are
proscribed; men slaughter each other at your very doors; they
die by hundreds, by thousands, fighting for or against an idea;
this idea calls itself good or evil; and you, continuing the while
to call yourselves men and Christians, would claim the right of
remaining neutral? You cannot do so without moral degradation. Neutrality, that is to say, indifference between good and
evil, the just and the unjust, liberty and oppression, is simply
Atheism.

Let us, then, endeavour to distinguish all that there is of permanent from all that is merely accessory and transitory in the
crisis; all that will remain, and which demands satisfaction,
from that which is only a momentary ebullition, the dross or
scum of metal in fusion. The question is now, how to bring
forward the balance of half a century which has passed to the
credit of the half century to come. We shall endeavour to do
this as rapidly as possible; not as summarily, however, as their
Excellencies the ambassadors of France, Austria, Russia, and of
the thirty-five or thirty-six States of Germany.

Their Excellencies have very recently made a discovery which
would remarkably simplify our solution if we could believe them
upon their word. According to them, there are in London four
or five persons who are the cause of all the disturbances of the
Continent; they walk abroad, and all Europe is agitated; they
associate themselves for an object, whatever it may be, and the
whole of Europe associates itself with them. We have only to
abandon the noblest privilege which we possess, that of exer-
cising a free hospitality, and to drive them across the ocean,
and Europe would sleep in peace under the bâton of Austria,
the knout of Russia, the *cavalletto* of the Pope. Pity that
Lord Granville should not have reached to the height of their
Excellencies! Pity that for such a peace he should scruple to
violate English law and English honour!

No; the agitation in Europe is not the work of a few individuals, of a few refugees, be they who they may; and there is
something in this opinion sad and ridiculous at the same time:
we say sad, because it evidently shows the inability of the
" masters of the world" to comprehend and to abridge the crisis.
Individuals are only powerful now so far as they are the expo-

nents of the condition and the collective aspirations of large
bodies of men. For sixty years Europe has been convulsed by
a series of political struggles which have assumed all aspects by
turns, which have raised every conceivable flag, from that of
pure despotism to that of anarchy, from the organization of the
bourgeoisie in France and elsewhere as the dominant caste, to
the *jacqueries* of the peasants of Gallicia. Thirty revolutions
have taken place. Two or three royal dynasties have been
engulfed in the abyss of popular fury. Nations have risen, like
Greece, from the tombs where they had been for ages buried;
others, like Poland, have been erased from the map. Forgotten,
almost unknown races, the Sclavonian race, the Roumaine race,
silent until now, have disinterred their traditionary titles and
demanded to be represented in the Congress of Nations. Kings
and Queens have gone to die in exile. The Austrian Empire,
the China of Europe, has been on the brink of destruction. A
Pope, drawn along by the popular current, has been obliged to
bless a national insurrection, and then to fly under favour of
disguise from the capital of the Christian world. Vienna has
twice been covered with barricades. Rome has seen the republican banner float above the Vatican. Governments, attacked
and overthrown, have ten, twenty times recovered strength,
drawn closer their alliances, overrun the half of Europe with
their armies, annihilated revolutions, effaced by the sword, the
scaffold, prison and exile, entire generations of revolutionary
spirits, and crushed, as they term it, the hydra of disorder and
anarchy. The heads of the hydra have sprung up again fifty
for one; the struggle has recommenced at the foot of the scaffold of those who initiated it; the idea has gained strength
beneath the hammer on the anvil: we are now, three years after
an European restoration, three months after the *triumph of order*
in France, calculating upon and arming for new struggles; and
we are told that all this is the work of a few individuals, trans-
mitting from one to another, every ten years, the inheritance of
a subversive idea! As well might the conquest of the world by
Christianity be attributed to the underground labour of a secret
society. Christian truth emerged from the catacombs, because
the whole world was thirsting for it. The ancient unity was
broken; a new one was necessary. Between these two unities
chaos reigned, in which humanity cannot live. It reigns now,
because, amidst the ruins of an unity in which there is no longer
any faith, a new unity is being elaborated. If a few men have
power with the multitudes, it is that these men embody this
unity in themselves better than all others. But though you may
destroy them to-day, others will replace them to-morrow.

Europe no longer possesses unity of faith, of mission, or of aim. Such unity is a necessity in the world. Here, then, is the secret of the crisis. It is the duty of every one to examine and analyze carefully and coolly the probable elements of this new unity. But those who persist in perpetuating, by violence or by jesuitical compromise, the external observance of the old unity, only perpetuate the crisis, and render its issue more violent.

Europe—we might say the world, for Europe is the lever of the world—no longer believes in the sanctity of royal races; she may still accept them here and there as a guarantee of stability, as a defence against the encroachments of some other dangerous element; but she no longer believes in the *principle*, in any special virtue residing in them, in a divine right consecrating and protecting them. Wherever they reign despotically, she conspires against them; wherever liberty exists under their sway, in however small a degree, she supports them under a brevet of impotence. She has invented the political axiom, "Kings reign without governing;" wherever they govern and govern badly, she overthrows them. Europe no longer believes in aristocracy, the royalty of several; she no longer believes in the inevitable physical transmission, in the perpetual inheritance of virtue, intelligence, and honour: she believes in it no longer, either scientifically or practically. Wherever an aristocracy acts well—if that ever happens to be the case—she follows its lead, not as an aristocracy, but as a doer of good; wherever it drags itself along in the pride of its old traditions—idle, ignorant, and decayed—she rids herself of it; she destroys it, either by revolutions or by ridicule. The carnival on the Continent looks to the historical order of patricians for its masks. Europe no longer believes in the Papacy; she no longer believes that it possesses right, mission, or capacity for spiritual education or guidance; she no longer believes in the immediate revelation, in the direct transmission of the designs and laws of Providence, by virtue of an election, to any individual whatsoever; five years ago she was seized with enthusiasm for a Pope who seemed disposed to bless the progress of the human race, and to constitute himself the representative of the most advanced ideas of his age; she despised him as soon as he retraced his steps and recommenced the brutal career of his predecessors. Europe no longer believes in privilege, be it what it may, except in that which no one can destroy, because it comes from God,—the privilege of genius and virtue; she desires wealth, but she despises or hates it in the persons of those who possess it, when it is not the price of labour, or when it arrogates to itself rights of political monopoly.

Now look at the organization of Europe—is it not altogether based upon privilege, by whatever name it may be known?

How then can one wonder at the struggle which is engendered within it?

Let it, then, be openly declared by every honest man, that this struggle is sacred, sacred as liberty, sacred as the human soul. It is the struggle which has for its symbol, since the commencement of the historical world, the great type of Prometheus; which has for its altar, in the midst of the march of the human race, the cross of Jesus; which has for its apostles almost all the men of genius, the thousand pillars of humanity. This war-cry which rises from the ranks of the Proletaire is the cry of our fathers, the Hussites: *The cup for all, the cup for all!* It is the logical consequence of the doctrine common to us all, the unity of God, and, therefore, of the human race. It is an effort to realize the prayer of Christ: *Thy will be done, on earth as it is in heaven!* Yesterday we worshipped the priest, the lord, the soldier, the master; to-day we worship MAN, his liberty, his dignity, his immortality, his labour, his progressive tendency, all that constitutes him a creature made in the image of God,—not his colour, his birth, his fortune—all that is accidental and transitory in him. We believe that every man ought to be a temple of the living God; that the altar upon which he ought to sacrifice to God is the earth, his field of trial and of labour; that the incense of his sacrifice is the task accomplished by him; that his prayer is love, his power—love realized—Association. We believe no more in that narrow dualism which established an absurd antagonism between heaven and earth, between God and his creation. We believe that the earth is the stepping-stone to heaven; that it represents a line in the immense poem of the universe, a note in the everlasting harmony of the Divine idea; and that on the accordance of our works with this harmony must depend the elevation of our actual being and our hope of progress in that transformation of life which we call death. We believe in the sacredness of individual conscience, in the right of every man to the utmost self-development compatible with the equal right of his fellows; and hence we hold that whatever denies or shackles liberty is impious, and ought to be overthrown, and as soon as possible destroyed. This it is which is at the bottom of the ever-recurring struggle in Europe; this it is which prevents either armies, or persecutions, or *coups-d'état* from conquering it, and which will insure final triumph.

Now, if around this idea which we have pointed out, fatal errors, vain or absurd desires, false and immoral systems, have been gathered, is it a reason for denying—not the errors, the immoderate desires, the systems, but—the idea itself? Is the religious idea an impious thing because heresies have been engrafted upon it? Shall we deny God because the Father of all has been transformed by the monk of the Inquisition into a universal tyrant? Shall the ravings of sceptical minds make us renounce the inviolable rights, or the power of human reason?

Such reactions take place only in weak and cowardly natures —for we do not address here men who choose their part through interested and selfish motives. We repeat that it is the duty of every honest and sincere man to study with impartiality the true causes of this prolonged crisis which embraces two-thirds of the populations of Europe, to range himself openly on the side of justice, to combat with the same energy enemies and false friends,—atheists and heretics, those who deny the right of progress, and those who falsify and exaggerate it. A faction must not be allowed to substitute itself for Humanity; but we must not, on the other hand, allow ourselves, through intolerance or fear, to *treat Humanity as a faction.*

We ask, is there one of our readers who can boldly say, " What you have just put forward as the final object of the European agitation is evil; we recoil from it"? No! Discussion may arise upon the means selected for its realization, upon the time, more or less near, of success; not upon the essence, upon the thing, upon the idea itself.

But around this holy aspiration towards the emancipation of oppressed classes and peoples, around this great social thought which ferments in all men's minds, there has arisen such an uproar of discordant and irritated voices, such a jumbling together of petty systems, of fragmentary conceptions, representing in reality nothing but individualities excited by vanity and morbid exaltation, that the aspiration, the primitive thought, has become obscure to our eyes. We have mistaken the glare of meteors for the true and steadfast light; we have forgotten what is principal in what is accidental and accessory; we have turned from eternal TRUST for the possible *realities* of a day.

To some the poniarding of Rossi has appeared to be the programme of the Italian revolution; while others believe that the French revolution and the abolition of all individual property are synonymous. These men forget one thing—the revolution itself; that of 1848, which confiscated nothing, which abolished no right; that of Rome in 1849, which slaughtered none but the foreign soldiers upon its walls. In what we have just indicated there is much more than a simple, an accidental contrast—there is the indication of a constant fact, of which those who seek in good faith to appreciate the crisis should never lose sight; the radical and habitual difference between the language of parties and their acts, between the excited exaggerated ebullitions of intelligence seeking conquest and brutally repulsed by force, and its practice, its point of view when it descends into the arena of action. Proudhon in power would not organize anarchy. There is hardly an intelligent communist who, on the morrow of a revolution, would take for his programme the ideal which he had preached before; there is not one of the preachers of systematic terrorism who, invested with power, would not recoil from the application of the rules which he had promulgated in defeat. This is in the nature of things. Besides the change which takes place in the same men in different positions, besides the difference between the unrestrained impulses of the writer or the propagandist orator, and the course, regulated by all external circumstances, of the legislator or the representative, there is the fact, that the work of preparation falls mostly into the hands of factions, whilst the practical solution of the crisis belongs to the mass, to the majority of the country. Now, the mass, the majority, never desires the impossible. It feels that it is called upon to continue, not to create Humanity. It takes tradition as its starting point; it advances, but does not break the chain; it is bound by too many habits and affections to the past. If you had fifty revolutions in Europe, not one would essay to establish communism or terror as a system. Those whom the reading of a pamphlet or an article of a paper inspires with alarm for property or for any other historical element of society, are the *enfans niais,* as the writers themselves are the *enfans terribles,* of our times.

This view is confirmed by facts. The republicans organized, under the reign of Louis Philippe, in the Society of the *Rights of Man,* affectedly designated their different sections by the names of Robespierre and Marat. The republicans in 1848 commenced by abolishing capital punishment for political offences; property was respected; and all the acts of the triumphant party were characterized by moderation. The Italian revolutions followed the same course. The powers which issued from insurrection in Hungary, at Vienna, throughout Europe, may have committed errors; they never sullied their career with spoliation or with blood.

But besides this puerile fear, which shuts its eyes to the approaching dawn, because of the fearful phantoms which the night evokes, there exists a general prejudice, alluded to some pages back, which radically vitiates the judgments brought to bear upon the European crisis. That error consists in this, that in seeking an insight into the issue of the crisis, and the tendencies which will govern its latest stage, attention is directed exclusively to France. Some seventy years ago, we used to judge all republican ideas by our historical recollections of Sparta and Athens; now we judge all that is called liberty, equality, association, by the meaning given, or thought to be

given, to these words in France. From continually fixing our
eyes upon Paris, we are no longer capable of seeing or comprehending the rest of Europe—of Europe gifted with an individual
life, with an individual organism, of which Paris is only one
amongst many centres of activity.

This arises from an idea which we believe to be false, and
which, consciously or unconsciously, prevails everywhere;
namely, that in France is the initiative of the continental
European movement.

In reality this initiative no longer exists.   A powerful
influence is naturally and inevitably exercised by a nation of
thirty-five millions of men, placed in a central position, endowed
with warlike habits, compact, centralized, the most decidedly
One amongst European nations.   But the initiative of ideas,
the moral and intellectual initiative—that which adds a new
element to the powers of civilization, or changes the general
point of view of the labours of Humanity—the initiative exercised by the discovery of the New World, by the invention of
the Press, by that of gunpowder, or by the application of steam
—the political initiative which leads to a social transformation,
to the emancipation of an enslaved class, to the study of a form
of new organization—has never been appropriated by any single
nation,—by France less than by any other.   Like the flaming
torches, the *lampada vitæ*, which were passed from hand to
hand, in the sacerdotal ceremonies of ancient Rome, it has
passed from one nation to another, consecrating them all mis-
sionaries and prophets of Humanity. Were they not all destined
hereafter to become brothers, fellow-labourers, equals, each
according to his especial capabilities, in the great common
workshop of Humanity, towards a common end,—collective
perfectionment, the discovery and progressive application of the
law of life? It has caused the idea of the divine Omnipotence
to spring from the old eastern world; human individuality from
the pagan Greco-Roman world, and more lately from the forests
of old Germany; the equality of souls from the doctrine
preached at Jerusalem; the democratic constitution of the City
from the Tuscan and Lombard republics; commercial association
from Bremen and the Hanseatic Towns; the colonizing idea
from England; the sacredness of human conscience from Germany; the pre-consciousness of the unity of Europe, and of the
world, twice from Rome; Art from Greece and Italy; Philosophy from all. If there is anything in this sunlike movement
of the human mind which characterises France, it is not the
initiative, it is rather the *popularization* of ideas. French
intelligence creates little; it assimilates much. It is essentially
constructive; the raw material comes to it from elsewhere.

Supple, pliant, active, full of self-confidence, instinctively mono-polizing, and aided by a language clear, facile, fitted for all conversational requisites, the French mind seizes upon ideas already put forth, but too often neglected elsewhere; it fashions, ornaments, appropriates them, and throws them into circulation; often facilitating that circulation by breaking up the idea, by dividing it into fragments, as we multiply our small coinage for the benefit of the greater number. Its life, its utility, is there; and it answers to this special function, which would seem to have been assigned to it, with an *aplomb de maître* and a con-fidence which insures success.

Il prend son bien où il le trouve; it refashions it, deals with it as it only knows how, and so well that other nations often receive from it in exchange that which they themselves had originated. It is not the less true, however, that the power of initiation, of spontaneous creation, which gives a new impulse to the mind when it seems exhausted, is not, exceptions apart, the innate faculty of the French nation. She called herself, in the first period of her history, *the arm of the Church;* she has often been since the *tongue* of the thought of others. Without her, perhaps, this thought would have long remained silent and sterile.

It is from the great Revolution of 1789 that we may date this prejudice in favour of France, whom the Peace of Utrecht had robbed of all preponderance. The bold defiance which she then threw, in the name of a great human truth, to the powers that were, the gigantic efforts by which she maintained it against the coalesced governments of old Europe, followed by the military glories of the Empire, are still working on the imagination of Europe. We all worship the echo, a little also the fact of power; and the remembrance of the great battles which led the French eagle from Paris to Rome, from the Escurial to the Kremlin, fascinates us as the image of a power which cannot die. The French Revolution has been regarded by all, historians and readers, as an European programme, as the commencement of an era; and as a conse-quence of this conception we see a series of secondary initiatives assigned to the people who gave the first. Every idea originat-ing in France appears to us fatally destined to make the tour of Europe.

This conception is, in our opinion, erroneous. What we say is grave indeed; for it would tend to change entirely the point of view of all appreciations of the events of this century. Differing in this respect from all writers on the Revolution, it would be necessary for us to develop our ideas at greater length than our present space permits. We could not, however, in

writing upon present European tendencies, avoid expressing a
conviction which would completely modify, supposing it to be
sound, our judgment upon these tendencies and their future.
We must ask our readers to supply this deficiency by a fresh
study of that revolutionary period, in the hope that we may find
an opportunity, perhaps in examining the recent histories of the
French Revolution, to bring forward our proofs.

The great French Revolution was not, philosophically speaking, a *programme;* it was a *résumé.* It did not initiate, it
closed an epoch. It did not come to cast a new idea upon the
world, to discover the *unknown quantity* of the problem of a
new era; it came to place upon a practical ground, in the
sphere of the political organization of society, a formula comprehending all the conquests of twenty-four centuries, all the
great ideas morally elaborated by two historical worlds, the
Pagan and the Christian world, of which, if we may allow ourselves the expression, it has brought down the balance. It took
from the Pagan world its declaration of liberty, of the sovereign
moi; from the Christian world its declaration of equality, that
is to say, of liberty for all, the logical consequence of the unity
of nature in the human race; hence also it derived its motto of
fraternity, the consequence of the Christian formula, *all men
are the sons of God;* and it proclaimed—and herein consists its
merit towards Europe—that all this ought to be realized here
below. Further than this it did not go. As in every great
summing up of the progress of the past, we can find the germ
of that of the future, the Revolution was marked by many
aspirations towards the idea of association, of a common aim,
of a collective solidarity, of a religious transformation,—which
idea dominates the present time; but in its official acts, in the
ensemble of its march, in its most characteristic manifestations,
it has never gone beyond the circle of progress already accomplished, the emancipation of *individuality.* This is why, after
having embodied its idea in a Declaration of the *Rights* of
man, of the individual, it was capable of ending with a man,
—with Napoleon. *Right,* that is to say, the individual as-
serting himself, was its life, its soul, its strength. *Duty,* that
is to say, the individual submitting himself to the idea of a collective aim to be attained, has never been its directing thought;
it was but the obligation, the necessity of fighting for the conquest of the rights of each; it made, so to speak, duty subser-
vient to rights. It never rose in action to the height of putting
forward a Declaration of Principles. Its definition of Life has
always been, whatever efforts may have been made to pass
beyond it, the materialist definition—*the right to physical well-
being.* It is so even now. And, nevertheless, Europe is now

agitated and unconsciously led by that other eminently religious definition—*life is a mission*, a series of duties, of sacrifices to be accomplished for others, in view of an ulterior moral progress.

France has, by its Revolution, borne witness in the civil world to the truths taught in the kingdom of souls by Christianity. She also has said, Behold the man: *Ecce homo.* She has laid down the principle of human individuality in the plenitude of its liberty in face of her enemies; and she has overthrown them all. She has done, politically, the work of Luther; here is her glory and her strength. But she has not given the Word of the future, the aim of the individual upon earth; she has not indicated the work to be accomplished, of which liberty is only a necessary premise — the new definition of Life which is to be the starting point of an epoch. Her great formula, which the imitative mind of democracy has rendered European, *liberty, equality, fraternity,* is only an historical formula, indicating the stages of progress already attained by the human mind. Now, every philosophical and social formula ought to contain, if it pretends to give a new initiative to the nations, an indication of the Law to be followed and of its necessary interpreter. The formula which the Italian Revolution inscribed upon the republican banner at Rome and Venice, GOD AND THE PEOPLE, is more advanced and more complete than that of the French republicans.

Since 1815, there has been a great want in Europe—the *initiative* has disappeared; it belongs to no country at the present time, to France less than to any other. Europe is in search of it; no one knows yet by which people it will be seized.

We must not, then—and this is the practical result which we are desirous of reaching—judge of the agitation, the aspirations, the tendencies of Europe, by France. France does not lead; she is only a member of the European commonwealth, simply one link in the chain.

There are in Europe two great questions; or, rather, the question of the transformation of authority, that is to say, of the Revolution, has assumed two forms : the question which all have agreed to call social, and the question of nationalities. The first is more exclusively agitated in France, the second in the midst of the other peoples of Europe. We say, *which all have agreed to call social*, because, generally speaking, every great revolution is social, in this, that it cannot be accomplished either in the religious, political, or any other sphere, without affecting social relations, the sources and the distribution of wealth. But that which is only a secondary consequence in political revolutions, is now the cause and the banner of the movement in France. The question there is now, above all, to establish better relations between labour and capital, between production and consumption, between the workman and the employer.

It is probable that the European initiative, that which will give a new impulse to intelligence and to events, will spring from the question of nationalities. The social question can, in effect, although with difficulty, be partly resolved by a single people; it is an internal question for each, and the French Republicans of 1848 so understood it, when, determinately abandoning the European initiative, they placed Lamartine's manifesto by the side of their aspirations towards the organization of labour. The question of nationality can only be resolved by destroying the treaties of 1815, and changing the map of Europe and its public Law. The question of *Nationalities*, rightly understood, is the Alliance of the Peoples, the balance of powers based upon new foundations, the organization of the work that Europe has to accomplish.

We should be wrong, however, to separate the two questions; they are indissolubly connected. The men who plead the cause of the Nationalities well know that revolutions, necessarily supporting themselves on the masses, ought to satisfy their legitimate wants; they know that a revolution is sacred whenever it has for its object the progress of the millions, but that it is an unpardonable crime when it has only for its object the interest of a minority, of a caste, or of a monopoly; they know that the problem now to be resolved is, the association of all the faculties, of all the forces of humanity towards a common end, and that no movement can at the present time be simply political.

By dividing into fractions that which is in reality but one thing, by separating the social from the political question, a numerous section of French socialists has powerfully contributed to bring about the present shameful position of affairs in France. The great social idea now prevailing in Europe may be thus defined: the abolition of the proletariat; the emancipation of producers from the tyranny of capital concentrated in a small number of hands; re-division of productions, or of the value arising from productions, in proportion to the work performed; the moral and intellectual education of the operative; voluntary association between workmen substituted gradually and peacefully, as much as possible, for individual labour paid at the will of the capitalist. This sums up all the reasonable aspirations of the present time. It is not a question of destroying, abolishing, or violently transferring wealth from one class to another; it is a question of extending the circle of consumers, of consequently augmenting production, of giving a larger share to producers, of opening a wide road to the operative for the acquisition of wealth and property, in short, of putting capital and the instruments of labour within reach of every man offering a guarantee of good will, capacity, and morality. These ideas are just; and they are destined eventually to triumph; historically, the time is ripe for their realization. To the emancipation of the *slave* has succeeded that of the *serf;* that of the serf must be followed by that of the *workman.* In the course of human progress the patriciate has undermined the despotic privilege of royalty; the bourgeoisie, the financial aristocracy, has undermined the privilege of birth; and now the people, the workers, will undermine the privilege of the proprietary and moneyed bourgeoisie; until society, founded upon labour, shall recognise no other privilege than that of virtuous intelligence, presiding, by the choice of the people enlightened by education, over the full development of its faculties and its social capabilities.

These ideas, we repeat, are not exclusively French; they are European. They are the result of the philosophy of history, of which the seeds sown by the Italian Vico have been cultivated more particularly by the German philosophers. From the moment that the human race was regarded not only as an assemblage of individuals placed in juxtaposition, but as a collective whole, living a providentially progressive life, and realizing an educational plan which constitutes its law, the series of terms composing the civilizing progression of which we spoke a little while ago, ought to suffice, by showing the conquests of the past, to point out the necessary progress of the future. The belief in the unity of the human race, and in progress, considered not as an accidental fact, but as *law,* would naturally beget modern democracy; belief in the collective life of society would lead to the idea of association, which colours all the efforts of modern reformers. The failure of ten revolutions lost by the bourgeoisie did the rest. It was shown that nothing now succeeds if not supported by the masses; and this support is only to be obtained by working evidently for them, by giving them an interest in the triumph of the revolutionary idea. Upon the practical ground, the existence of standing armies sold body and soul to absolutism has materially assisted in enlarging political programmes, and in impressing them with a popular and social tendency. It was necessary to find a power to oppose to this mute and blind force, which crushed ideas under the heavy step of battalions in rank and file; where could it be found if not in the people? The men of the party of progress addressed themselves to it, some through faith, others through policy, through necessity; all learned to know it, to feel for what it was ripe, by seeing it in action. Action is the thought of the people, as thought is the action of the individual. It was a sudden revelation confirming all the presentiments of science, all the aspirations of faith. Justice and duty call upon us to proclaim aloud that upon the barricades as in their passive resistance, after the victory as during the struggle, wherever they were not momentarily led astray by ambitious or mistaken men, the people acted bravely and nobly. The blouse of the workman revealed treasures of devotion, of generosity, of patience, suspected by none. At Paris, at Milan, at Rome, at Venice, in Sicily, in Hungary, at Vienna, in Poland, everywhere, the populations gave the lie, by their conduct, to the terrors excited by what was called the unchained lion. There was neither massacre, pillage, nor anarchy. Before the signs of a great idea, at the words *Country, Liberty, Independence,* the cry of misery itself was silent. Sublime words were spoken, as by the Paris workmen, when they said, " we can suffer four months of hunger for the republic;" there were sublime acts, as the pardon granted by the people of Milan to Bolza, the man who had been their persecutor for twenty-five years, " because to pardon was a sacred thing." The women of the Transtevere at Rome, lodged by the Government, at the time of the bombardment, in the palaces of the exiled nobles, upon the simple promise, in the name of " God and the people," that they would commit neither theft nor injury, kept their word religiously. The people of Berlin took no other revenge for the four hundred and twenty-one victims who had fallen under the troops, on the 18th of March, 1848, than that of burning, without taking a single article, the furniture of two traitors, Preuss and Wernicke. Men who had never been included in the ranks of democracy, as Lamartine and Victor Hugo, were converted by the combatants of Paris. Even Pope Pius the Ninth was himself, for a moment, fascinated.

Principles and facts, theory and practice, thus united to prove to the men who believe in progress and are willing to act for it, that the object of their efforts ought to be, and can be without difficulty at the present time, the people in its totality, irrespective of propertied or privileged classes. And as it is impossible to dream of the moral and intellectual progress of the people, without providing for its physical amelioration—as it is absurd to say, " *instruct yourself,*" to a man who is working for his daily bread from fourteen to sixteen hours a day, or to tell him to *love* who sees nothing around him but the cold calculations of the speculator and the tyranny of the capitalist legislator, the social question was found inevitably grafted upon the question of political progress. Henceforward they cannot be separated but by destroying both.

But in Italy, in Hungary, in the states composing the empire of Austria, in Poland, in Germany, the social question presents nothing of a threatening, subversive, or anarchical nature. There is no hostile, profoundly reactionary sentiment between class and class, no exaggerated abnormal development of concentrated industry, no agglomerated misery rendering urgent the instant application of the remedy, no reckless putting forth of systems and solutions. Communism has made proselytes amongst the workmen of Germany; but this ebullition, produced by a thoughtless reaction against the weakness of the revolutionary direction in 1848, is not of serious moment; with the exception of Marx, who was desirous of being the chief of a school at any price, there is not a single man of any intelligence who has given in to the notion that Communism can be established by enactment. Generally, the men who are destined to have an influence upon events believe that association must be voluntary; that it is the duty of Government to encourage, but not to impose it. The chief exceptions are found in France. Here, the question which with the other peoples is secondary, and rather the *means* than the *end*, has acquired a preponderating importance and peculiar characteristics. The special condition of interests, the existence of large manufacturing centres, the shamelessness with which the bourgeoisie has confiscated to its own advantage two revolutions made by the people, the absence of the question of national unity,—so absorbing for the other nations, and already irrevocably conquered in France,—the enthusiasm, to a certain extent factitious and transient, with which the French mind seizes upon every novelty, have all contributed in that country to give to the ideas which we have laid down a character of exclusiveness and exaggeration which they are unlikely to assume elsewhere.

French *Socialism* has forcibly stirred men's minds; it has raised up a number of problems of detail of which there was no suspicion before, and of which the solution will have a certain importance in the future; it has—and this is a positive benefit— excited a searching European inquiry into the condition of the working classes; it has uncovered the hidden sores of the system founded upon the spirit of caste and monopoly; it has incited the bourgeoisie to a reaction so ferocious and absurd, that its condemnation, as a governing caste, is consequently assured at no distant period. But it has falsified and endangered the great social European idea, raised up innumerable obstacles to its progress, and created against it furious enemies, where it ought naturally to have found friends—in the small bourgeoisie; it has

kept numbers of intelligent men from entertaining the urgent
question of liberty; it has divided, broken up into fractions, the
camp of democracy, for the union of which an ample field of
conquests, already morally won, was assured. The French Socialists deny this; but for every impartial mind the state into
which France has fallen must be an argument which admits of
no reply.

France is still profoundly materialist, not in the aspirations of
her people whenever they are collectively manifested, but in the
majority of her intellectual men, her writers, her statesmen, her
political agitators. She is so almost in spite of herself, often
even without knowing it, and believing herself to be the contrary.
She talks of God without feeling Him, of Jesus while dressing
him up in the robe of Bentham, of immortality while confining
it to the earth, of European solidarity while making Paris the
brain of the world. The philosophy of the eighteenth century still
possesses her. She has changed her phraseology, but the thing,
the parent-idea, remains. She is still commenting, under one
disguise or another, on the dogma of *physical well-being*, the
law of *happiness*, which the catechism of Volney drew from
Bentham.

Analysis has almost destroyed in France the conception of
life. The faculty of synthetical intuition, which alone gives us
the power of embracing it in its unity and comprehending its law,
has disappeared with the religious sentiment, giving place to a
habit of dividing into fractions an intellectual question, and of
fastening by turns upon one only of its manifestations, thus
taking a part for the whole. Mind has become again in some
sort polytheistical. Every man is a formula, every formula a
fragment of the civilizing synthesis. You have mystics, mate-
rialists, eclectics; not a single philosopher. You meet with
Fourierists, Communists, Proudhonians; very few French republicans, making the republic a symbol of all progressive development. French intelligence attaches itself exclusively to
one face of the moral polyhedron. Each secondary end becomes for it the great end to be attained; each remedy for a
malady an universal panacea. The school of St. Simon recognised in history only *critical* and *organic* epochs; it defamed
the one and admired the other, forgetting that every epoch is
critical in relation to the preceding one, *organic* in relation to
itself or to the future. Other schools establish a perpetual antagonism between religion and philosophy, without ever suspect-
ing that philosophy accepts the fall of one belief only on condition of preparing the way to a new one, and that, generally,
the substantial difference between religion and philosophy is this,
that the latter is—when scepticism is not taken for philosophy—

the religion of the individual, whilst the former is the philosophy of the many, of collective humanity. This tendency to cut up into fragments that which ought to harmonize as a whole, is the radical vice of French *Socialism*. It has torn up the banner of the future, and each school, seizing upon one of the fragments, declares it to be the whole. Each word of the device, *liberty, equality, fraternity,* serves, separated from the other two, as the programme for a school. Each of the two great unalterable facts, the individual and society, is the soul of a sect, to the exclusion of the other. The individual, that is to say, liberty, is destroyed in the Utopia of St. Simon, in the communism of Babeuf, and in that of his successors, by whatever name they call themselves. The social aim disappeared in Fourierism ; it is openly denied by Proudhon. It would seem that it is not given to the French to understand that the *individual* and *society* are equally sacred and indestructible, and that it is the manner of reuniting and harmonizing these two things which is the aim of all the efforts of the present time.

Life is one : the individual and society are its two necessary manifestations; life considered singly and life in relation to others. Flames from a common altar, they approach each other in rising, until they unite together in God. The individual and society are sacred, not only because they are two great *facts*, which cannot be abolished, and which, consequently, we must endeavour to conciliate, but because they represent the only two *criteria* which we possess for reaching our object, the truth, namely, *conscience* and *tradition*. The manifestation of truth being progressive, these two instruments for its discovery ought to be continually transformed and perfected ; but we cannot suppress them without condemning ourselves to eternal darkness; we cannot suppress or subalternize one, without irreparably mutilating our power. Individuality, that is to say, conscience, applied alone leads to anarchy ; society, that is to say, tradition, if it be not constantly interpreted, and impelled upon the route of the future by the intuition of conscience, begets despotism and immobility. Truth is found at their point of intersection. It is forbidden, then, to the individual to emancipate himself from the social object which constitutes his task here below, and to society to crush or tyrannize over the individual ; and, nevertheless, if we examine the basis of the French *socialist* systems, we shall find nearly all of them defective in one or other of these respects.

This system of dismembering that which is essentially one has produced its effect in the actual state of things. French democracy has separated itself into two camps, that of politics and that of socialism. The occupants of the first call themselves

men of revolutionary tradition, the others, prophets, or apostles
of social reform. This has produced an absurd antagonism between the men who said, *Let the nation be free, she shall then
judge between us all;* and the men who, shutting themselves
up in a vicious circle, said, *The nation cannot be free, unless she
adopt our system*—the vanity of the Utopist substituting itself
for the collective thought. Some sects have advocated indifference to the questions of organization of power, pretending that
the social transformation could take place under any form of
government. Other fractions of the party have replied by re-
acting violently against every *socialist* idea; by refusing the
co-operation of all those who declared themselves believers in
any given system; and by exaggerating to themselves the
danger of some exclusive views, destined to disappear submerged in the first storm of the popular ocean. Others, again,
fearing the exactions of the working classes led astray by the
doctrines of the Utopists, have desired to avoid the danger at
any price, and have preached to the people during three years,
as their best policy, peace, abstention from every manifestation, that of the electoral urn excepted. The bourgeoisie,
systematically threatened, pointed out, as a hostile power, to
the indignation of the working classes, fell back towards the
status quo, fortifying itself in the sphere of government; the
people reacted against it by organizing itself for insurrection.
Anarchy entered the ranks. A man, gifted with a disastrous
and terrible logic applied to a false principle, and powerful upon
weak minds by his incredible audacity and by a clear and cutting rhetoric, came to throw the light of his torch upon this
anarchy, and took it for his motto, with a laugh. Proudhon,
an anti-socialist, summed up in himself all the phases of socialism. He refuted one system by another; he killed off the chief
of one sect by another; he contradicted himself ten times over.
He enthroned Irony as queen of the world, and proclaimed the
Void. It is in this void that Louis Napoleon has entered.

We have said that the first cause of this anarchical disorder
of French socialism is the materialism which still governs the
mind of the country. This is so true, that the worship of
material interests has become its watchword. We know the
exceptions, and we honour them, but they do not destroy the
general fact. The great and noble question of the perfectibility
of collective humanity, and the emancipation of the classes who
are excluded from educational progress by the desperate struggle
which they are obliged to maintain for the means of material
existence, has been narrowed by the majority of French socialists
to the proportions of a problem of industrial organization. That
which ought only to be the indispensable *means*, has become in

their hands the final *object.* They found man mistrustful, hostile, egotistical, and they thought to soften and improve him by an increase of wealth. Doubtless they have not denied the religion of the soul, but they have neglected it; and in fixing, almost exclusively, the attention of the masses upon their material interests, they have assisted in corrupting them; they have, instead of destroying its source, enlarged the foundation of egotism in extending it from the bourgeoisie to the people. St. Simonianism, that is to say, the school which felt so strongly from the first the unity of humanity, that it had made its programme a religious one, finished by the worship of *happiness,* by what it termed the *rehabilitation of the flesh,* by the identification of the *peaceful* epoch of the future with the *industrial* one. Its disciples are to be found, nearly all of them, at the present time in the ranks of the existing power, whatever it may be. Fourier, still bolder, denied morality, and gave *pleasure* as the watchword of progress, legitimized all human passions, and materialized the soul by a degrading theory of enjoyment. Communism gave, as its foundation for society, men's wants; it was ever speaking of the right to happiness; it made the abolition of individual property the secret of the regeneration of the world. Proudhon, hastening to abandon the destructive character and to produce something organic, placed at the summit of the social pyramid, in the place of God, a bank of gratuitous credit. The worship of material interests spread from the chiefs to their subalterns, to the commonalty of the party, exaggerated, intolerant, vindictive, and exclusive. They continued, in the name of the red republic, the dissolving, corrupting task of Louis Philippe. They spoke of money, when they ought to have stirred up souls in the name of the honour of France; of property to be acquired, when they ought to have spoken of duty; of hatred to the bourgeoisie, whilst military dictatorship was at their doors. They now gather the bitter fruits of their error; some of them even avow it; others are only prevented from so doing by an inexcusable vanity.

Man is not changed by whitewashing or gilding his habitation; a people cannot be regenerated by teaching them the worship of enjoyment; they are not led to sacrifice by speaking to them of material rewards. It is the soul which creates to itself a body, the idea which makes for itself a habitation. The Utopist may see afar from the lofty hill the distant land which will give to society a more virgin soil, a purer air; he ought to point it out with a gesture and a word to his brothers; but he cannot take humanity in his arms, and carry it there with a single bound; even if this were in his power, humanity would not therefore have progressed.

Progress is the consciousness of progress. Man must attain it step by step, by the sweat of his brow. The transformation of the *medium* in which he lives only takes place in proportion as he merits it; and he can only merit it by struggle, by devoting himself and purifying himself, by good works and holy sorrow. He must not be taught to enjoy, but rather to suffer for others, to combat for the salvation of the world. It must not be said to him, *Enjoy, life is the right to happiness;* but, rather, *Work; life is a duty, do good without thinking of the consequences to yourself.* He must not be taught, *to each according to his wants,* or *to each according to his passions,* but rather, *to each according to his love.* To invent formulas and organizations, and neglect the internal man, is to desire to substitute the frame for the picture. Say to men, *Come, suffer; you will hunger and thirst; you will, perhaps, be deceived, betrayed, cursed; but you have a great duty to accomplish:* they will be deaf, perhaps, for a long time, to the severe voice of virtue; but the day that they come to you, they will come as heroes, and will be invincible. Say to them, *Arise, come and enjoy; the banquet of life awaits you; overthrow those who would prevent you from entering:* you would make egotists who would desert you at the first musket-shot, such as those who, the day after having cried *Vive la République,* vote for Louis Napoleon, if he but makes them tremble, or if he promises them to mingle a few grains of socialism with his despotism.

It is the instinctive belief in these things which renders the cause of the nationalities powerful and sacred. It is by this worship of the idea, of the true, of the morally just, that, in our opinion, the initiative of European progress belongs to them.

It was not for a material interest that the people of Vienna fought in 1848; in weakening the empire it could only lose power. It was not for an increase of wealth that the people of Lombardy fought in the same year; the Austrian Government had endeavoured in the year preceding to excite the peasants against the landed proprietors, as they had done in Gallicia; but everywhere they had failed. They struggled, they still struggle, as do Poland, Germany, and Hungary, for country and liberty, for a word inscribed upon a banner, proclaiming to the world that they also live, think, love, and labour for the benefit of all. They speak the same language, they bear about them the impress of consanguinity, they kneel beside the same tombs, they glory in the same tradition, and they demand to associate freely, without obstacles, without foreign domination, in order to elaborate and express their idea, to contribute their stone also to the great pyramid of history. It is something moral which they are seeking; and this moral something is at the bottom, even politically speaking, the most important question in the present state of things. It is the organization of the European task. It is no longer the savage, hostile, quarrelsome nationality of two hundred years ago which is invoked by these people. The nationality which Ancillon founded upon the following principle—*whichever people, by its superiority of strength, and by its geographical position, can do us an injury, is our natural enemy; whichever cannot do us an injury, but can by the amount of its force and by its position injure our enemy, is our natural ally,*—is the princely nationality of aristocracies or royal races. The nationality of the peoples has not these dangers; it can only spring from common effort and a common movement; sympathy and alliance ought to be its consequence. In principle, as in the ideas formally laid down by the men influencing every national party, nationality ought only to be to humanity that which the division of labour is in a workshop, the recognised symbol of association, the assertion of the individuality of a human group called by its geographical position, its traditions, and its language, to fulfil a special function in the European work of civilization.

The map of Europe has to be re-made. This is the key to the present movement; here lies the initiative. Before acting, the instrument for action must be organized; before building, the ground must be one's own. The social idea cannot be realized under any form whatsoever before this reorganization of Europe is effected, before the peoples are free to interrogate themselves, to express their vocation, and to assure its accomplishment by an alliance capable of substituting itself for the absolutist league which now reigns supreme.

Take the map of Europe. Study it synthetically in its geographical structure, in the great indications furnished by the lines of mountains and rivers, in the symmetrical arrangement of its parts. Compare the previsions of the future which this examination suggests, with the existing collocation of the principal races and idioms. Open the page of history, and seek for the signs of vitality, for the different populations, resulting from the *ensemble* of their traditions; listen, in short, to the cry which rises from the consciousness of these populations through their struggles and their martyrs. Then observe the official governmental map, such as has been sanctioned by the treaties of 1815. In the contrast between these two you will find the definitive answer to the terrors and complaints of diplomatists. Here is the secret of the *conspiracy* which they are endeavouring to destroy, and which will destroy them. Here also is the secret of the future world.

It is in these thirteen or fourteen groups, now dismembered

into fifty divisions, almost all weak and powerless before five of
them possessing an irresistibly preponderating force. It is in
this Germany, now divided into thirty-five or thirty-six States, a
prey alternately to the ambition of Prussia and Austria, and
which knows no other divisions than those of pure Teutonic
nationality in the south and of Saxony in the north, united on
the line of the Maine. It is in this immense race, whose out-
posts extend as far as Central Germany in Moravia, which has
not yet uttered its national cry to Europe, and which aspires to
say it—in heroic Poland, whom we have so much admired only
to forget her at the moment of her downfall—in the Sclavonia
of the south, extending its branches along the Danube, and
destined to rally itself in a vast confederation, probably under
the initiative of Hungary—in the Roumaine race, an Italian
colony planted by Trajan in the lower basin of the Danube,
which would appear to be called upon to serve as a bridge of
communication between the Sclavonian and the Greco-Latin
races. It is in Greece, which has not risen from the tomb where
it lay buried for ages to become a petty German viceroyalty,
but to become, by extending itself to Constantinople, a powerful
barrier against the European encroachments of Russia. It is in
Spain and Portugal, destined sooner or later to be united as an
Iberian peninsula. It is in the ancient land of Odin, Scandi-
navia, of which Sweden must some day complete the unity. It
is above all in Italy, a predestined nation, which cannot resolve
the question of its independence without overthrowing the empire and the papacy at the same time, and raising above the
Capitol and the Vatican the banner of the inviolability of the
human soul for the whole world.

We have not space for all that we would fain say upon this
subject of the nationalities, of which the importance is as yet
unrecognised in England. We would willingly trace the first
lines of the study which we have pointed out; we would willingly apply the deductions arising from it to each of the countries which we have just named, and plunge into the details of
the movement which has, since a certain number of years, acquired a practical value. This we cannot now do. But we affirm
with profound conviction, that this movement only just initiated
for some of the groups, already far advanced for the others, has
attained for Italy, for Hungary, for Vienna, for a great part of
Germany, and for some of the Sclavonian populations, a degree
of importance, which must, at no distant period, produce
decisive results. It is probable that the initiative of these events
will spring from Italy; it is already ripe; but let it come from
where it may, it will be followed. An isolated national revolution is no longer possible. The first war-cry which arises will

carry with it a whole zone of Europe, and through it Europe herself. It will be the epopee of which 1848 has been the prologue.

In the face of this crisis, which every day brings nearer to us, what is England doing and what ought she to do?

What she is doing is this. She lives from day to day bandied about between a policy pretending to renew the alliance of the smaller against the menaces of the larger States, supporting itself upon a *moderate* party destitute of intelligence, energy, or strength—a policy which has no meaning when the question is between to be and not to be; and another policy which shamelessly says to the country, *We will play the spy for the sake of the established Governments.* The first timidly hesitates between that which is and that which will be; it caresses Prussia, condemned to impotence between terror of Austria and of German democracy; it seeks an ally against Austria in the Piedmontese monarchy, twice crushed at Milan and at Novarra, and which would inevitably be so a third time if it ever dared to defy again its enemy; it urges the established Governments to concessions, it recoils from their logical consequences; it irritates despotism without weakening it; it raises the hopes of the populations without realizing them; it must meet hatred from some, incredulity from others. The second openly retraces its steps towards absolutism. Both have brought England to the abdication of herself in the affairs of Europe; they are bringing her sooner or later to absolute isolation. Self-abdication and isolation: is that a life worthy of England? Are nations no longer allied, as individuals are, by duty? Ought they not to do good and to combat evil? Are they not members of the great human family? Do they not live the life of all? Ought they not to communicate something of their life to all? Can they remain strangers to the common task of leading mankind towards perfection, the realization of the educational plan assigned to humanity? And have we the right of uttering the name of religion, when crime is committed at our very doors which we could prevent, and when we cross our arms in indifference? In 1831, we proclaimed the duty of non-intervention as the basis of European international relations. It was an irreligious and negative principle: we ought to intervene for good; we ought not to be able to intervene for evil. And yet this principle, coming between the two opposing elements, might be intelligible as a means of arriving at the true condition of the peoples and their capacity of realizing the progress which they invoke. How has it been maintained? Wherever nations have arisen to organize themselves in a manner more suitable to their present belief and interest, Prussian, Austrian, or French despotism has

employed its brute force upon each isolated people; England
has not even protested upon the tombs of Rome and Hungary.
The menace of the foreigner weighs upon the smaller States;
the last sparks of European liberty are extinguished under the
dictatorial veto of the retrograde powers. England—the country
of Elizabeth and Cromwell—has not a word to say in favour of
the principle to which she owes her existence.

If England persist in maintaining this neutral, passive, selfish
part, she must expiate it.   European transformation is inevitable; when it shall take place, when the struggle shall burst
forth at twenty places at once, when the old combat between
fact and right is decided, the peoples will remember that England has stood by an inert, immoveable, sceptical witness of
their sufferings and efforts.   Ancient alliances being broken, the
old States having disappeared, where will be the new ones for
England? New Europe will say to her, *Live thy own life.* This
life will be more and more restricted by the gradual inevitable
emancipation of her colonies.   England will find herself some
day a third-rate power, and to this she is being brought by a
want of foresight in her statesmen.

The nation must rouse herself, and shake off the torpor of her
Government. She must feel that we have arrived at one of those
supreme moments, in which one world is destroyed and another
is to be created; in which, for the sake of others and for her
own, it is necessary to adopt a new policy.

This policy is that of the nationalities, that which will protect
openly and boldly their free development; it is a great and a
useful policy.

There is evidently an attempt at universal restoration in
Europe. From Vienna it has passed to Rome; from Rome to
Paris. Where will it stop? It is now hanging over Switzerland, Piedmont, and Belgium; it tends to suppress liberty, the
press, the right of asylum. When that shall be accomplished,
when England shall be the only European land upon which
liberty, the press, the right of asylum, still exist, do you think
that an effort will not be made to destroy them there? No
army, perhaps, will succeed in landing upon her soil; but is it
by invasion only that a country is destroyed? The Holy Alliance
renewed, has it not ports to close, obstructions to oppose to
travellers? Can it not forbid the introduction of our press, spread
papal corruption, sow divisions between class and class, excite
revolts in our colonies? We arm, we authorize rifle-clubs, we
speak of militia; we are then in fear; and yet we repulse the
most efficient means of safety that Europe offers us; we leave
the people who would be our nearest allies to fall one by one
under the attacks of *la terreur blanche;* we renounce, with a

fatal obstinacy, the glorious rôle which the loss of the French initiative yields to the first nation willing to seize upon it, a rôle which would assure us the first influence in the Europe of the future, safety from all attempts against liberty, and the consciousness of the accomplishment of a duty towards the world. National defences ! Our national defences against the Court of Rome are in Rome herself delivered from French occupation, that living insult to civilized Europe, which has no other object now than that of holding, in contempt of every right, a strategic position in Italy ; our best defence against Austria is in Milan, at Venice, in Switzerland, in Hungary; against Russia, in Sweden, in Poland, in the Danubian Principalities; against France, in the alliance of the young nationalities which will shortly furnish her with the opportunity of awakening and of overthrowing that imperialism which now threatens us, because an army is its slave, with the most dangerous enterprises.

Within the last two or three months a voice has reached us from across the Atlantic, saying, *Evil is being done daily in Europe, we will not tolerate its triumph, we will no longer give Cain's answer to God who has made us free ; we will not allow foreign armies to suppress the aspirations which we hold sacred, the ideas which may enlighten us. Let every people be free to live its own life. To maintain this liberty we are ready to intervene by word of mouth,—if need be, by the sword.* This cry, rising from the majority of the population, and from a part of the official world in the United States, is directed to us. It comes from a branch of our own race. Let us accept it, and rebaptize our alliance by a policy worthy of us both. There is something great in this idea of an Anglo-American alliance coming from the lips of an exile. The laying of the first stone of that religious temple of humanity which we all foresee, is a labour well worthy the co-operation of the two worlds. We hope, nay, we believe, that there are many English hearts which echo the wishes and convictions lately uttered by one of the greatest of American statesmen, Daniel Webster. Speaking of the relations between England and the United States, he says:—

" Instead of subject colonies, England now beholds a mighty rival, rich, powerful, intelligent, like herself. And may these countries be for ever friendly rivals. May their power and greatness, sustaining themselves, be always directed to the promotion of the peace, the prosperity, the enlightenment, and the liberty of mankind; and if it be their united destiny, in the course of human events, that they shall be called upon in the cause of humanity, and in the cause of freedom, to stand against a world in arms, they are of a race and of a blood to meet that crisis without shrinking from danger, and without quailing in the presence of earthly power." *

---

* Address delivered before the New York Historical Society, Feb. 23, 1852.

LA

DERNIÈRE GUERRE

ET

LA PAIX DÉFINITIVE EN EUROPE

PAR

VICTOR CONSIDERANT.

Prix : 15 centimes.

PARIS

LIBRAIRIE PHALANSTÉRIENNE, QUAI VOLTAIRE, 25, ET RUE DE BEAUNE,

—

1850.

IMPRIMERIE LANGE LÉVY ET COMP., RUE DU CROISSANT, 16.

LA DERNIÈRE GUERRE

ET

LA PAIX DEFINITIVE EN EUROPE.

I.

La prochaine guerre, qui sera la dernière, se fera, comme toutes les guerres, avec du canon, sans doute ; mais, dans cette guerre, le canon ne tiendra qu'un rang subalterne.

Les principes, les sentiments et les idées seront l'artillerie décisive de cette lutte suprême.

Les préparatifs en sont gigantesques. Jamais l'Europe n'a porté un pareil poids de soldats. Du Rhin au Volga, les armées du despotisme couvrent la terre comme les vapeurs du matin.

Pour que ces armées se fondent en quelques heures aux rayons de la liberté, pour que la Démocratie sociale triomphe universellement et miraculeusement, il suffit d'une chose : c'est 'que la Démocratie ne se trahisse pas elle-même, qu'elle se montre partout fidèle à ces principes : Association et Liberté.

Aujourd'hui, plus véridiquement qu'au temps de l'assassin couronné qui donna son nom à Constantinople, un *labarum* brille au ciel de l'Europe, gage certain de victoire. Sur ce *labarum*, cinq mots sacrés sont écrits :

TOUS LES PEUPLES SONT FRÈRES.

C'est le principe de la Démocratie sociale, son idée supérieure, sa synthèse.

Ces mots sortent de l'Evangile.

C'est le principe chrétien, passé de l'ordre simple à l'ordre composé, la formule évangélique élevée à sa seconde puissance.

C'est la fraternité sociale, la fraternité des nations et des races, corollaire collectif de la fraternité des individus.

Tout est prêt pour une explosion européenne de cette religion nouvelle.

LES LEÇONS DE DIEU.

La Providence, qui est l'histoire en action, la loi vivante du développement de l'humanité, vient de faire aux Peuples un cours complet ; rien n'y manque. Les leçons ont été rudes ; elles ont profité aux élèves. Peuples, bénissez les verges : leurs coups vous ont ouvert les yeux.

En 1831, la Pologne veut briser le joug moscovite. Malgré des prodiges d'héroïsme, elle dut reprendre ses fers. Ce fut justice. Cette révolution militaire et aristocratique avait dédaigné le peuple. L'aristocratie polonaise, les Czartoriski et consorts, refusèrent aux démocrates de décréter l'émancipation des serfs. Au lieu d'avoir affaire à un Peuple, le czar n'eut qu'une armée à vaincre. Les conservateurs de l'esclavage retombèrent en esclavage. Ce fut justice. Vaincu, le parti aristocratique polonais a dû confesser sa faute. Il proclame lui-même aujourd'hui, dans l'émigration, la légitimité de l'affranchissement des paysans. — Et d'une.

La Démocratie était maîtresse de Vienne le

6 octobre 1848. Dans les conditions qu'elle fit à l'Empereur, la Diète autrichienne sacrifia à des moyens termes l'affranchissement de l'Italie, et ne stipula que pour elle-même. La Démocratie a été vaincue à Vienne. — Et de deux.

La Diète de Francfort, qui voulait la liberté et l'unité de l'Allemagne, s'accommoda de la domination de l'Allemagne sur l'Italie. La Diète de l'unité allemande s'est misérablement évanouie. — Et de trois.

La Hongrie, qui voulait la liberté pour elle, n'avait pas toujours respecté celle des Slaves et des populations roumanes enclavés dans son empire. Kossuth lui-même, le grand Kossuth commit au début la faute de tergiverser sur l'affranchissement de l'Italie, et, un moment, fit à demi cause commune avec Radetzki. Les Slaves de Jellachich ont été les premiers agresseurs de la Hongrie, et la république hongroise a succombé sous les armes unies du slavisme russe et des égorgeurs de l'Italie. — Et de quatre.

Les Croates se sont mis, contre la Hongrie, au service du despotisme de la maison d'Autriche. Ils regimbent aujourd'hui dans les serres de l'aigle impériale. — Et de cinq.

Les Polonais et les Allemands, un moment unis en 48, cédant à des excitations machiavéliques contre lesquelles des démocrates devraient se tenir en garde, se divisent et se font une guerre fratricide dans le duché de Posen. Allemands et Polonais retombent sous le joug de leurs anciens maîtres. — Et de six.

Enfin, les représentants officiels de la révolution française de 48, de cette révolution qui avait charge de Peuples, qui avait révolutionné les autres Peuples, qui leur avait promis aide et appui, ces républicains officiels, mus par le sot espoir de se faire accepter dans la communion européenne des grands amis de l'ordre (féodal), ont trahi les engagements de la Révolution et livré les Peuples. Si bien que la République, aux mains de la réaction royaliste à l'intérieur, est enveloppée aujourd'hui par les forces coalisées de la réaction européenne. — Et de sept.

C'EST BIEN FAIT !

Tous les égoïsmes ont reçu leur châtiment, et chacun de ces châtiments est une leçon utile. Peuples, bénissez les verges ! Vous avez manqué de charité sociale ; vous avez failli aux devoirs de solidarité ; vous avez faibli dans la foi, et vous avez été frappés de plaies cruelles. Ne dites pas que Dieu vous a abandonnés : vous vous êtes fort bien abandonnés vous-mêmes. Vous êtes instruits.

LA MORALE DES LEÇONS.

Les privilégiés, les aristocrates, les empereurs et les rois ont compris, eux, leur solidarité. Partout ils se sont entendus, concertés, soutenus. Ils ont agi en Europe comme un seul homme, et partout ils nous ont vaincus.

La formule de la Démocratie sociale, le mot sacré de l'Ordre nouveau, c'est ASSOCIATION, — Association des individus, des familles, des Peuples et des races.

Association implique LIBERTÉ pour tous et FRATERNITÉ de tous envers tous.

Tant que vous ne respectiez pas la liberté des autres peuples comme vous voulez que l'on respecte la vôtre ; tant que vous n'étiez pas prêts à secourir les autres peuples et à défendre leurs droits comme vos propres droits, vous n'étiez encore vous-mêmes que des aristocrates, des dominateurs, tout au moins des égoïstes. Vous n'étiez dignes ni de la Liberté ni de l'Association. Bénissez les verges de Dieu ! Elles vous ont appris que vous ne pouvez rien les uns sans les autres. Elles ont fait de tous les Peuples un seul Peuple, de toutes les Démocraties une seule Démocratie.

Un mot se lit aujourd'hui, de Berlin à Rome, tracé sur le sol européen en lettres gigantesques, avec des gibets, des tombes et des centaines de mille cadavres italiens, français, allemands, russes, hongrois, polonais ; ce mot est SOLIDARITÉ. C'est le résumé des sept leçons de la Providence, la morale de ses sept coups de verges.

Ce mot, il ne suffit pas qu'il soit écrit sur le sol sanglant, il faut qu'il soit gravé dans tous les cœurs.

Il faut plus ; il faut que tous les publicistes et tous les orateurs de la Démocratie universelle, tous ceux qui préparent par le Verbe la victoire de la Liberté, traduisent la foi dont ce mot est le symbole dans toutes ses formules concrètes, en déduisent et en vulgarisent toutes les applications.

Le but immédiat de la Démocratie, le fait magnifique qui jaillira du sein des peuples de l'ancien monde, sous l'inspiration du Socialisme, après le prochain ébranlement, c'est la constitution harmonique de l'Europe, l'Unité par la Liberté, la libre confédération de toutes les nationalités affranchies, petites ou grandes, et conséquemment l'inauguration de la PAIX PERPÉTUELLE.

De quel droit un peuple prétendrait-il se soustraire à la tyrannie d'un autre peuple ou d'une maison princière, s'il entendait opprimer lui-même, sous quelque prétexte que ce fût, une nationalité quelconque, si faible que soit celle-ci ?

Arrière donc le prétendu droit historique, qui n'est que le droit féodal, le droit de conquête, l'oppression prolongée !

II.

A LA BOURGEOISIE.

—

L'ORDRE FÉODAL EUROPÉEN.

Les rois, les maisons princières, les intérêts aristocratiques et le droit du canon, seuls jusqu'à nos jours, ont fait la carte politique du monde. Aussi le monde n'a-t-il connu qu'un ordre arbitraire, faux, opposé aux tendances naturelles des populations, par conséquent violent, par conséquent instable.

Un ordre, construit par le jeu des ambitions féodales et monarchiques, qui opprime les sympathies les plus saintes, les plus vivaces des peuples, est sans cesse miné par la conjuration des forces vives sur lesquelles il pèse. C'est la guerre en permanence, latente ou patente, c'est le DÉSORDRE servant de base à un ordre arbitraire.

Ce DÉSORDRE doublé de force, c'est pourtant ce que les meneurs de la réaction osent appeler aujourd'hui l'ORDRE EUROPÉEN !

Le maintien de cet ordre faux, compressif, arbitraire, exige, année commune, deux millions d'hommes armés en Europe et dévore deux milliards !

Dans les temps difficiles comme aujourd'hui, c'est plus de trois millions cinq cent mille soldats qu'il lui faut, et plus de trois milliards cinq cent millions qu'il absorbe !

Ce n'est pas tout. Ces trois millions cinq cent mille hommes, enrégimentés pour la tuerie, le service des princes, le maintien de l'ordre violent, sont, en force et en activité, l'élite des populations laborieuses; ils perdent à ne pas produire au moins autant qu'ils dépensent pour s'exercer à détruire.

C'est donc plus de SEPT MILLIARDS, autrement dit soixante-dix fois cent millions, la rente d'un capital de 140 milliards, que l'agriculture, l'industrie, le commerce, la propriété et le travail sacrifient annuellement, en Europe, à quoi ? — Au maintien de l'Ordre européen ?—De quel Ordre européen ?—D'un ordre européen selon les vœux et les intérêts des Prussiens, des Autrichiens, des Polonais, des Russes, des Slaves méridionaux, des Hongrois, des Français, des Italiens, de tous les peuples du continent enfin ? — Nullement. Au contraire !

Eh pardieu ! c'est précisément parce que l'Ordre européen des rois a contre lui tous les peuples qu'il faut sept milliards pour l'entretenir, pour le défendre, et qu'il faut trois millions cinq cent mille hommes pour l'imposer par violence aux populations qui conspirent incessamment contre cet ordre oppressif.

Si l'Ordre européen était conforme aux volontés et aux intérêts des peuples, s'il était l'expression même de la liberté, il se maintiendrait de lui-même. L'Ordre du despotisme coûte sept milliards aux peuples par an. L'Ordre de la liberté ne leur coûtera rien.

Ces trois millions cinq cent mille hommes, ces sept milliards sacrifiés annuellement par la propriété et le travail, ces milliers de forteresses à entretenir, ces milliers de bastions à couvrir de canons, ces arsenaux de guerre à remplir, tout cela pour les intérêts de la famille royale de Prusse, de la maison impériale d'Autriche, de sa majesté le czar de toutes les Russies, d'une quarantaine de princes, principules et principicules d'Allemagne, et de deux ou trois grands ou petits ducs en Italie... C'est bien la peine !

L'ORDRE DÉMOCRATIQUE EUROPÉEN. — UNE HYPOTHÈSE.

Ecoutez-moi un moment, ô vous débonnaires bourgeois de France et d'Allemagne. Je m'adresse à ceux d'entre vous qui se sont laissé prendre aux filets de la Réaction; écoutez-moi. Parlons net, sans passion, sans emportements. Tâchons de nous rendre compte des choses, de réfléchir et de raisonner un peu.

Tenez ! je suppose qu'un Pouvoir supérieur, un génie céleste, un Archange, tout ce que vous voudrez de plus élevé dans l'administration de la République du bon Dieu, transporte aujourd'hui, tout vivants et avec les honneurs dus à leur rang, dans le giron du Très-Haut, les empereurs, rois, princes et ducs ci-dessus désignés, et avec eux leurs familles, leurs valets, leurs menins, leurs courtisans et tous ceux de leurs grands officiers qui voudraient les suivre... Soit quinze cents ou deux mille familles royales, féodales, aristocratiques, dont le continent se trouverait ainsi tout à coup privé.

A cette nouvelle, je vous entends :

« Quel évènement ! quel malheur ! quelle si-
» tuation ! quel bouleversement ! que va devenir
» l'Europe ! Plus de rois, plus de princes... La
» société est détruite, les peuples sont perdus ! »

Le premier étonnement passé, vous vous rassureriez un peu. Quelqu'un d'entre vous ne tarderait pas à dire :

« Ah bast! après tout la terre tourne toujours
» sur son axe d'Occident en Orient ; le soleil se
» lève tous les matins aux heures de mon alma-
» nach ; le grain mûrit, les arbres poussent, la
» pluie tombe, tout va comme devant. Le bon Dieu
» l'a voulu, nous nous passerons de princes. Et,
» ma foi ! continuons nos affaires. »

Voici maintenant que l'Archange, son expédition terminée, nous revient, et parle à l'Europe en ces termes :

« Peuples !

» Vous étiez jusqu'ici gouvernés et parqués comme d'augustes personnages entendaient que vous deviez l'être pour les intérêts de leurs maisons.

» Dès aujourd'hui, vous n'avez plus de listes civiles à payer à ces illustres familles. C'est un beau chiffre de millions que vous économisez. Mais cela n'est rien. Il vous appartient de vivre en paix et en prospérité. Vous êtes libres.

» Faites l'ORDRE sur la terre.

» Distribuez-vous et groupez-vous selon vos propres tendances, selon vos instincts de nationalité. Vous n'avez plus qu'à suivre vos affinités de races, de langages, d'intérêt, de religion. Vous êtes majeurs ; faites vos affaires.

» Il n'y a plus qu'un droit pour la Constitution des Etats. Ce droit a pour formule : *Liberté absolue de chaque groupe de population ;* il implique *respect absolu de la liberté d'autrui.*

» De la liberté seule peut sortir un classement parfait, un ordre naturel, et conséquemment inaltérable. Si vous demandiez à Dieu le Père de vous classer lui-même, de régler l'ordre et la carte politique de l'Europe, il ne pourrait que s'en rapporter à vous ; il vous répondrait : *Il y a dix-huit cents ans que je vous ai envoyé mon Fils pour vous enseigner ma loi :* AMOUR et LIBERTÉ. Groupez-vous librement et confédérez-vous fraternellement. »

L'Archange ayant ainsi parlé, toutes les nationalités se dégagent et s'organisent par leur propre spontanéité.

L'Italie, la Hongrie, la Pologne, secouant leur triple suaire, se lèvent dans la plénitude de la vie et de l'indépendance.

L'Allemagne constitue son unité.

Les Roumains (12 millions d'hommes de race latine), les Slaves méridionaux, les populations grecques, dégagés de la double pression russe et ottomane, constituent, de l'Adriatique au Dnieper, des Etats libres et confédérés.

De la Courlande à la Finlande, les riverains de la Baltique se réunissent à la famille scandinave dont ils ont été violemment disjoints.

En un mot, la carte politique de l'Europe se fait d'elle-même, conformément aux affinités ethnographiques. Expression libre de la volonté des populations, elle offre enfin l'ordre vrai, l'ordre naturel, l'ordre libre, l'ordre pacifique, l'ordre stable.

Je vous entends dire :

« Très bien ! mais il y faudrait l'Archange... »

Je vous réponds :

« L'Archange est là..... Son nom est DÉMOCRATIE. »

LA CAUSE DU MAL.

Il faut comprendre l'histoire et la philosophie. Les éléments en sont aujourd'hui si simples, qu'il y aurait mauvaise volonté à en méconnaître les enseignements. Les voici en deux mots :

L'Europe a été barbare.

La Barbarie, c'est la guerre, la force, la conquête.

Le régime de la conquête s'est organisé sous le nom de régime féodal.

Le droit féodal, c'était, non pas le droit des peuples, le droit de tous, le DROIT enfin, mais bien le droit du plus fort, le droit violent des conquérants, c'est-à-dire la négation même du droit.

Les droits des conquérants se sont concentrés dans les familles aristocratiques, princières, impériales, royales.

La constitution monarchique de l'Europe n'était donc que le dernier terme, la synthèse du régime barbare, conquérant, féodal.

Or, grâce au progrès, à la Science, à l'Industrie et à leurs deux principaux agents, l'imprimerie et la vapeur, l'idée, le droit et le travail ont gagné tout le terrain perdu par la force et par la guerre.

Tout était réglé, arbitrairement et violemment, par le jeu sanglant des armes, pour les intérêts d'ambition et de domination des familles féodales. Tout doit être désormais réglé par la liberté, pour les intérêts de travail et de bien-être des peuples.

L'Europe barbare, féodale, guerrière, avait une constitution monarchique, aristocratique, militaire.

L'Europe est devenue industrieuse. Il lui faut une constitution libre et pacifique.

Tout le mal vient donc de ce que la constitution barbare, féodale, s'impose encore par la force, par la pression de trois millions d'hommes armés, à l'Europe moderne, à l'Europe civilisée et industrieuse.

A l'Europe nouvelle il faut une constitution nouvelle.

LES INTÉRÊTS MODERNES.

Quels sont, je vous prie, les intérêts des peuples modernes ? Quel est leur but d'activité ? Sont-ils mus, comme jadis, par de brutales ambitions de conquêtes ? *Étranger*, dans les langues modernes, signifie-t-il encore *ennemi*, comme dans les langues anciennes ? Le peuple de France se sentirait-il possédé de la passion de subjuguer le peuple allemand, le peuple italien ? Ceux-ci, à leur tour, rêvent-ils l'envahissement de la France ? et ainsi des autres ?

Nullement ! Les peuples modernes veulent être libres et riches, travailler, produire, commercer, jouir. Ils se tendent les mains. Les temps sont bien changés ! L'idée du droit a jeté des racines profondes dans l'humanité. Victimes séculaires de la force, les peuples invoquent le droit. L'Europe industrieuse a soif de paix, d'accord et de liberté !

Donc, propriétaires, industriels, commerçants, vous tous qui composez la bourgeoisie laborieuse et active de tous les pays, quand vous examinez l'état militaire de l'Europe ; quand vous voyez du détroit de Gibraltar à la Néva, trois millions cinq cent mille hommes en armes ; quand vous réfléchissez que cela vous prend annuellement sept milliards, si vous vous demandiez pourquoi tant de bataillons et de millions, vous pourriez vous répondre : « Nous payons ce » monstrueux tribu de sept milliards pour donner » aux familles féodales les moyens de maintenir » violemment sur l'Europe industrieuse, sur l'Eu- » rope moderne, malgré les peuples, la vieille » constitution du pouvoir féodal, militaire, bar- » bare, qui attribue les peuples à ces familles.

» Nous payons ou perdons annuellement sept » milliards pour entretenir la révolution en Eu- » rope ; car tant que les peuples seront opprimés » par la constitution arbitraire qui les livre aux » familles impériales et royales d'Autriche, de » Russie et de Prusse, la liberté conspirera de » Rome à Varsovie, contre la domination vio- » lente de ces trois familles.

» Nous payons sept milliards, enfin, pour em- » pêcher les instincts de liberté et toutes les for- » ces vives de la société moderne, de donner à » la société moderne une constitution moderne, à » l'Europe industrieuse et civilisée, une organi- » sation libre, stable et pacifique. »

Et maintenant, industriels, commerçants, propriétaires et bourgeois de toutes les patries, pourriez-vous dire quel grand intérêt vous avez à ce que la maison d'Autriche retienne, malgré eux, sous son joug, les Italiens, les Hongrois, les Polonais, les Croates, etc. ?

Et quel grand intérêt vous avez à ce que la maison de Holstein Gottorp et les Boyards moscovites, retiennent malgré eux, sous leur joug, les Lithuaniens, les Finlandais, les Varsoviens, les Cosaques (qui détestent le joug russe, soit dit en passant), et pèsent sur les Valaques et les Moldaves !

Et quel grand intérêt encore vous avez à ce que trente ou quarante familles royales, ducales, archiducales ou grand-ducales, coupent l'Allemagne en trente ou quarante morceaux, entravent les rapports commerciaux des populations, et grugent celles-ci en prélevant sur elles des listes civiles véritablement fabuleuses!

Et quel intérêt vous avez à ce que le gouvernement exécré des prêtres soit imposé, par des baïonnettes et des gibets en permanence, à l'héroïque population romaine !

Pourriez-vous dire enfin quel intérêt vous avez à prolonger la révolution européenne, à retarder d'une ou de deux années la chute du système féodal radicalement incompatible avec l'Etat moderne de l'Europe, à charger les soupapes pour provoquer les explosions, à vous compromettre très gravement en soutenant la cause perdue des familles de la conquête qui n'est pas votre cause, mais celle de vos ennemis et de vos maîtres ?

Hommes de la bourgeoisie, conservez votre concours à la cause des familles féodales, vous voilà solidaires et compromis avec elles, en guerre contre les peuples avec elles, écrasés dans leur chute prochaine, inévitable.

Retirez-leur votre concours ; leur force tombe. Tout s'arrange pacifiquement, librement, fraternellement en Europe.

CE QUE VEUT LA DÉMOCRATIE SOCIALE.

Les démocrates ne veulent pas le désordre, comme les gens intéressés à ce que vous le croyez, vous le font accroire. Les démocrates veulent l'Ordre, l'Ordre vrai, naturel, libre et stable, l'Ordre européen conforme aux intérêts, aux besoins de l'Europe industrieuse ; l'Ordre contre lequel il ne se fera plus de révolutions parce qu'il ne sera plus oppressif.

Mettez-vous du parti de cet Ordre-là.

Cessez de soutenir l'ordre violent, faux, impossible, l'ordre suranné de la conquête, le vieil ordre féodal que vos pères ont sapé par la base ! faites-vous démocrates, et, je le répète, tout s'arrange pacifiquement, spontanément, fraternellement en Europe.

Les peuples indépendants et librement unis, travaillent, commercent, multiplient à l'infini les relations fécondes, et forment la grande confédération pacifique de la civilisation européenne, préludant ainsi à l'unité collective du monde. Les forteresses sont rasées, les remparts démolis, les frontières ouvertes, les armées licenciées ou converties en armées industrielles de la grande civilisation. Les sept milliards annuels du pied de guerre, que l'Europe paie à ses maîtres pour le maintien de l'ordre féodal et de la révolution, font retour à la propriété, au travail, au commerce. La guerre, la conquête, la barbarie sont enterrées, et l'ère de l'industrie, de la liberté et de la paix s'ouvre sur la terre aux chants de reconnaissance et d'amour des peuples et des races à jamais réconciliées et unies !

Des budgets écrasants, des banqueroutes-monstres, la conspiration européenne en permanence, des révolutions chaque printemps, et la guerre, la guerre, toujours la guerre, cela serait-il plus de votre goût ? préférez-vous que la lutte commencée depuis trois cents ans dans les esprits, par la science et l'industrie, contre la féodalité, glorieusement transportée par vos pères, les bourgeois de 89, sur le terrain civil et politique, il y a soixante ans; préférez-vous que cette lutte continue à déchirer les entrailles de l'Europe ? qu'elle s'envenime par votre résistance ? qu'elle se fasse implacable, surtout contre les traîtres de la révolution, et que le Peuple universel, au jour inévitable du jugement, vous écrase dans votre apostasie avec les tyrans et les tyranneaux dont l'égoïsme, la peur et la sottise vous auront fait les champions, les défenseurs et les complices ?

Préférez-vous cela à la liberté générale, à l'organisation naturelle de la confédération européenne, à la dissolution définitive de la guerre et des armées, à la constitution du système pacifique de l'Europe industrieuse, aux flots de richesses dont la science, le travail, le commerce couvriraient en quelques années le continent pour jamais uni et pacifié ?

Je sais bien que l'annonce de cette magnifique métamorphose du monde, de cette constitution de l'ordre vrai, fondé sur la liberté même des peuples, a le privilège d'exciter les grimaces railleuses des sceptiques, des empiriques, c'est-à-dire des grands hommes politiques de la réaction, de ses folliculaires faméliques et de beaucoup de niais qui se laissent encore enfenouiller par les affreux petits rhéteurs qui composent l'armée vénale, haineuse et verbeuse des aristocrates et des jésuites.

Je sais cela ; mais je sais aussi que le monde féodal, monarchique et barbare est mort. Je sais que le droit de la conquête et l'esprit de guerre ne sont plus ni l'esprit ni le droit de la société moderne. Je sais que tous les intérêts modernes de l'industrie, du commerce, du travail, de la liberté conspirent pour un ordre nouveau. Je sais que l'esprit de fraternité fermente dans les entrailles des nations, qu'une inextinguible ardeur d'indépendance les embrase ; que l'Italie veut être italienne, la Hongrie hongroise, la Pologne polonaise, les Slaves à eux, non à des maîtres étran-

gers, l'Allemagne à ses intérêts, à sa race, à son unité, non aux quarante sangsues princières qui la morcellent et la dévorent. Je sais que les Cosaques de l'Ukraine eux-mêmes abhorrent le joug des boyards et ensanglantent chaque jour l'ignoble knout moscovite qui les gouverne. Je sais que le vent de la liberté s'est levé sur l'Europe ! je sais que l'esprit de libre examen mord, dissout, mine et sape par toute l'Europe tous les pouvoirs imposés, violents qui n'ont pas leurs racines dans le droit, leur consécration dans la souveraineté de la nation ! Je sais que des peuples, qu'on croyait dégénérés, morts, ensevelis sous la pierre séculaire de l'oppression, se sont dressés fièrement à la face du monde, réclamant leur place au soleil de Dieu ! Je sais que leur noble sang fume encore sur les calvaires de leurs nationalités reconquises ! Je sais que si les oppresseurs ont pu sceller de nouveau sur eux la pierre du tombeau, si ces peuples sont redescendus au sépulcre, ils y sont redescendus vivants, et que, sous peu, ils en sortiront vivants !... Et la prochaine résurrection, je le sais encore, ne sera plus une résurrection de peuples isolés, mais de peuples unis, la résurrection européenne ! Voilà ce que je sais.

Non ! ce ne seront plus Rome, Milan, Venise, Vienne, Berlin, Pesth, Prague, Paris se levant sans s'entendre et se donner la main. Prochainement, au signal des rois du Nord, ou, s'ils n'osent, au signal de la France démocratique reprenant légalement et régulièrement possession d'elle-même, ce sera la démocratie européenne se dressant toute entière, se levant, parlant et agissant comme un seul homme ! Résurrection universelle, liberté de tous, liberté pour tous, libre confédération des peuples libres ! Place au droit, place aux peuples, place aux races, place à l'Ordre, à l'Ordre moderne, à la paix des nations, à la constitution de l'Europe civilisée et industrieuse !...

IL FAUT EN FINIR.

Les organes de la réaction crient tous les jours qu'*il faut en finir*.

Ils ont raison.

Oui, IL FAUT EN FINIR ! Voilà trois cents ans qu'a commencé la lutte de la liberté contre le despotisme. Depuis soixante ans, l'Europe n'est qu'une arène de sang et de révolutions, parce que le despotisme ne veut pas céder la place à la liberté. IL FAUT EN FINIR.

Il est certain, en effet, que l'industrie, le commerce, le travail et tout ce que l'on appelle les affaires ne sauraient marcher et prospérer au sein de cette anarchie, au milieu de ces éruptions sans cesse renaissantes du volcan de l'esprit moderne.

Féodalité, force brutale et Despotisme,—Liberté, Fraternité et Association :—il y a guerre, guerre implacable entre ces deux formules. Il faut choisir !

Quand je dis qu'il faut choisir, je n'entends point qu'il soit possible que le passé arrête le présent et étouffe l'avenir. Cela ne se peut pas. Le passé est mort : son esprit s'en est allé ; son cadavre seul pèse encore sur la société moderne. Ce n'est qu'une question d'enterrement. Ce cadavre nous empoisonne, et il faut choisir entre une inhumation immédiate, paisible, régulière, ou le prolongement de la peste qui sort de ce cadavre, avec combat aux les funérailles. Voilà ce que je veux dire.

C'est à la bourgeoisie française et à la bourgeoisie allemande à faire leur choix et à décider la question.

Bourgeois, laissez tomber le système féodal ; retirez votre appui à la réaction européenne, c'est-à-dire à la cause des trois familles impériales et royales du nord et de la valletaille des princes et rois subalternes de l'Allemagne et de l'Italie ; déclarez-vous pour l'ordre moderne, et TOUT SERA FINI !

La féodalité, le despotisme, l'esprit de domination et de conquête enterré, les armées licenciées, les impôts réduits de moitié, les peuples indépendants et unis, le droit de la force abattu, la révolution européenne accomplie, — les affaires, dans l'inébranlable système pacifique de l'Europe libre et confédérée, prendront des développements gigantesques, inouïs.

Industriels et commerçants, comprenez donc ceci :

Les nations libres sont des forces productives, des magasins de richesses sociales, des ateliers de travail et des comptoirs de commerce.

Les peuples asservis sont des forces révolutionnaires et des magasins à poudre toujours prêts à sauter.

Que l'Europe soit débarrassée de ses rois féodaux ! elle n'est plus conquérante, elle rase ses places fortes, licencie ses armées, travaille, prospère.

Quelle soit libre ! Elle n'est plus révolutionnaire ; car elle n'est révolutionnaire que pour conquérir la liberté.

Industriels et commerçants, ceux d'entre vous que la réaction européenne a entortillés dans ses filets et qu'elle y retient encore, sont de grandes dupes. Vous laisser enrôler au service de l'ordre féodal pour faire durer quelque temps encore la révolution et la guerre en Europe, et pour retarder d'autant l'avènement de l'Ordre régulier, de l'Ordre du travail, de l'industrie et de la liberté ! Vous ? vous, les fils des bourgeois de 89, au service de vos ennemis de douze cents ans, et cherchant à rapiécer les guenilles féodales qu'ont si bien mises en morceaux vos pères ?

Heureusement que vous vous instruisez ! Les actes furieux, les lâchetés, les violences impuissantes des amis de la modération échevelée et de l'ordre féodal vous ouvrent les yeux ! La dernière élection de Paris et les votes des départements sont là pour le dire. Bourgeois de France et d'Allemagne, il en est temps encore. En vous ralliant à la Révolution européenne qui vous a faits ce que vous êtes, que vous avez faite vous-mêmes, en assurant ses conquêtes, en l'accomplissant, en revenant à l'invincible parti de la liberté et des peuples qui est votre parti, vous pouvez encore conjurer les catastrophes, et faire avec les peuples, à coups d'opinions, ce que sans vous les peuples seront obligés de faire contre leurs implacables ennemis et contre vous-mêmes à coups d'insurrections.

Etes-vous pour la prolongation violente d'une organisation féodale, conquérante, militaire et barbare, superposée, dans l'intérêt de quelques famille aristocratiques et princières, à l'Europe industrieuse et civilisée ? ou pour une Constitution libre de l'Europe, pour la confédération pacifique des nations, pour l'établissement de l'Ordre convenant à la société moderne ? C'est toute la question. Quel que soit votre choix, la destinée s'accomplira. Mais, suivant ce que vous déciderez, vous serez vainqueurs avec elle ou elle sera victorieuse contre vous.

LA POLITIQUE MODERNE.

La grande politique n'est pas dans les bavardages de M. Thiers, de M. Molé, de M. Barrot et de toutes nos célébrités verbeuses.

Elle est dans le sentiment de la réalité vivante, dans la notion des besoins, des intérêts et des passions et des droits d'une époque.

Je dis que le premier démocrate venu, ouvrier, bourgeois ou paysan, dont la poitrine vibre quand on parle liberté et fraternité des peuple ; qui est prêt à s'aller faire tuer, s'il le faut, pour la liberté de l'Italie, de la Hongrie, de la Pologne, pour la cause de la démocratie européenne enfin ; je dis que celui-là, pour illettré qu'il puisse être, porte en lui cent fois plus de véritable science historique et politique que n'en contiennent toutes les têtes de nos poupées parlementaires. Celui-là, il est dans la réalité, dans l'histoire, dans la vie. C'est un homme en chair et en os, qui a du sang dans les veines, un cœur et une âme. Les autres sont des marionettes savantes, des automates de carton.

L'écolier qui sait que la terre et les planètes tournent sur elle-mêmes et autour du soleil, est cent fois plus fort en astronomie que ne l'étaient les plus habiles observateurs du ciel avant Copernik.

A bas le système féodal ! à bas la conquête et ce qui reste du droit de conquête ! à bas la guerre !

Hourra pour la liberté et la paix universelles, pour l'indépendance des nationalités et la confédération pacifique des peuples libres !

La vraie, la grande politique de l'époque est toute entière dans ce cri.

III.

A LA DÉMOCRATIE.

—

LA LIBERTÉ INTÉGRALE, PRINCIPE DE LA DÉMOCRATIE.

La dernière guerre sera la guerre de l'indépendance européenne. Elle anéantira le despotisme et tuera la guerre.

Pour que la Démocratie sociale ne commette plus de faute, pour qu'elle ne laisse aucune prise à la division dans ses rangs et qu'elle ne s'aliène aucun groupe, aucun élément de nationalité, il faut qu'elle se pénètre profondément de son but supérieur et du caractère de la constitution européenne qui se dégagera de la dernière lutte.

Ce caractère, ce sera l'Unité, non plus l'unité forcée, l'unité violente, mais l'UNITÉ PAR LA LIBERTÉ.

Quand la France eut, en 92, à défendre la Révolution et les principes de l'ordre moderne contre la coalition au dehors et la trahison au dedans, elle dut s'organiser en guerre. Son unité dut être l'unité d'une armée.

Devant l'ennemi, le fédéralisme, c'est-à-dire les libertés locales, c'était la division, la faiblesse, l'envahissement de la France, la ruine de la Révolution.

Il fallait sauver la France et la Révolution. A ce besoin suprême, souverainement légitime, on sacrifia sans hésiter toutes les libertés : liberté communale, liberté départementale ; on supprima même les provinces. On fit bien.

Lorsque le système féodal sera détruit en Europe, les peuples libres, les armées dissoutes, les places fortes ouvertes, remparts rasés, la guerre et l'esprit de conquête éteints, et qu'une Diète démocratique européenne aura dans ses attributions e règlement des rares difficultés internationales

qui pourront survenir entre peuples — les libertés locales ressusciteront partout dans la sécurité générale, au sein de l'unité fédérative du continent.

C'est parce qu'ils ont conscience de cette grande Unité, libre et fédérative, que les vrais démocrates socialistes haïssent toute esprit de conquête, repoussent toute adjonction violente, et même toute ambition d'accroissement de territoire.

Un soir, M. de Lamartine, étant encore membre du gouvernement de la République, j'eus avec lui, sur les affaires étrangères, une conversation d'où j'appris qu'il convoitait pour la France la Savoie et le comté de Nice, offrant la Lombardie à la Sardaigne, et rendant la Venetie à l'Autriche (1). Ce fut un éclair. J'avais nourri avec amour de grandes illusions sur le barde de la Démocratie. Ce mot fit tomber les écailles qui couvraient mes yeux. Je reconnus avec douleur que l'esprit de l'avenir n'avait pu se dégager, pur et libre, de l'esprit du passé, dans cette harpe d'or. L'avenir brillait dans les dytyrambes du poète, le passé gouvernait les pensées et les tendances de l'homme politique. Lamartine était perdu pour la Révolution. Faute de foi dans la grandeur des destinées de la Démocratie sociale et du monde moderne, il tourbillonnait entre les deux courants. Il devait bientôt y sombrer.

Quiconque en France, aujourd'hui, rêve pour la France, l'ébranlement prochain de l'Europe, un agrandissement quelconque, un pouce de terre pris à des voisins, celui-là peut être un impérialiste, un républicain de l'ancien *National* (école hybride qui n'existe plus) ; à coup sûr il n'est pas un démocrate, encore moins un démocrate socialiste.

Introduire un grain d'égoïsme dans le sentiment démocratique, c'est se faire empoisonneur public.

Le despotisme n'a plus qu'une force morale en Europe. Cette force est indirecte, et n'est pas à lui. C'est celle qu'il tire de l'antagonisme machiavéliquement entretenu et attisé entre les peuples, des divisions et des irritations qu'il exploite.

Les maisons impériales d'Autriche et de Russie, les deux seuls ennemis sérieux de l'ordre moderne, ne subsistent qu'en opprimant, les unes par les autres, les nationalités diverses qu'elles opposent sans cesse et lâchent les unes sur les autres comme des bêtes de combat.

Diviser pour dominer, voilà la devise du passé, des intérêts monarchiques, de la barbarie.

---

(1) Je considère comme une chose tellement malheureuse pour M. de Lamartine d'avoir conçu et caressé une pareille idée, que je n'eusse jamais parlé de ce projet, s'il n'eut été révélé déjà dans plusieurs publications.

S'unir pour être libres, voilà la devise de l'avenir, des intérêts démocratiques, de l'ordre vrai, du régime de paix, de travail, d'accord, de richesse générale et de fraternité.

Le premier parmi les peuples apôtres de la démocratie, c'est aujourd'hui le peuple français. Son caractère d'initiateur lui impose une loi, et c'est cette loi qui maintiendra sa grandeur. Il doit être le serviteur de tous les peuples, même des plus petits, surtout des plus petits.

Il est deux écoles grotesques dont les derniers débris, en France et en Allemagne, doivent tomber sous les sifflets combinés de la démocratie des deux pays :

En Allemagne, l'Ecole historique et féodale, qui réclame l'Alsace, la Lorraine et les Pays-Bas. Démocrates allemands, sifflez vos don Quichottes teutons, vos farouches Gallophages.

En France, l'Ecole des culottes de peau, les cacochimes de l'Empire, les vieilles bêtes qui, prenant la guerre pour l'état normal de l'Europe moderne parce qu'elle a été l'état normal de l'Europe barbare, croient sincèrement que la France ne saurait se passer des frontières des Alpes et du Rhin. Il leur faut Nice et la Savoie, Genève, les provinces Rhénanes et la Belgique, pour raison de sûreté. Et puis, cela fait bien sur la carte. M. Thiers en est. Démocrates français, sifflons ces vainqueurs.

Lorsque l'Allemagne aura constitué son unité par la République, que la Pologne, la Hongrie, l'Italie, les Slaves méridionaux seront libres et confédérés avec les Républiques démocratiques de France et de Germanie, qu'importeront, je vous prie, les questions de frontières ?

Il n'y aura plus de frontières armées et fermées.

Il y aura des groupements naturels et volontaires, de petits et de grands Etats, des provinces européennes unies, ouvertes aux rapports scientifiques, industriels, artistiques et commerciaux des peuples associés et vivant en frères, indissolublement liés par un réseau gigantesque et infiniment ramifié de routes, de canaux, de chemins de fer, de communications de toutes sortes, qui formeront de Cadix à Pétersbourg l'arbre veineux et artériel du grand corps européen. Dans ce corps, il y a des organes divers, il n'y a plus d'ennemis.

La démocratie sociale n'a que trois ennemis à combattre, la Tyrannie, la Guerre et la Misère. Ces trois furies sont sœurs et leurs destins sont liés. Abattez l'une, les deux autres tombent du même coup.

Proclamons donc hautement, radicalement, intégralement notre principe, LA LIBERTÉ ! la liberté sans réserve, la liberté par tous et pour tous, la liberté des faibles aussi bien que celle des forts, la liberté des faibles protégées par les forts.

LIBERTÉ INTÉGRALE, INTÉRÊT DE LA DÉMOCRATIE.

. La liberté n'est pas seulement le principe primordial de la démocratie, c'est encore son intérêt le plus sérieux. *On a souvent besoin de plus petit que soi*, a dit excellemment le fabuliste ; ronge-maille le rat peut quelquefois délivrer le lion du filet ou l'y laisser captif.

Quand la croisade du despotisme marchera sur le foyer de la démocratie sociale, elle entendra bien, malgré leur neutralité, passer sur le corps de la Suisse et de la Belgique.

S'il ne nous importe pas d'avoir la Suisse et la Belgique à nous, il nous importe beaucoup de ne les avoir contre nous ni l'une ni l'autre.

Bonaparte avait détenu la Belgique et violé la Suisse. Il avait pris à celle-ci Genève et Lausanne. Il avait donné Neuchâtel à l'un de ses lieutenants, et imposé à la diète le joug de fer de son protectorat. En 1814 et en 1815, la Belgique et la Suisse s'ouvrirent d'enthousiasme aux alliés. Ce fut bien fait. Bonaparte a eu dans les reins des balles suisses et des balles belges, des balles de tous les peuples qu'il a voulu dominer, quand il aurait pu les rendre libres. Certes, il les avait méritées ces balles. Il pouvait être le Washington de l'Europe, il aima mieux étouffer la liberté, éventrer sa mère la République, se faire le gendre de l'empereur d'Autriche, fabriquer des ducs, des rois, des comtes, des barons, s'harnacher en Louis XIV et en Charlemagne, tout cela au dix-neuvième siècle, après 89, après 93 ! ! Que la démocratie lui pardonne, car il a compris ses fautes et confessé la Démocratie et la République universelle à Sainte-Hélène. Que les démocrates aussi comprennent bien les leçons de l'histoire. L'antipode de la démocratie c'est la violence. Plus rien contre le droit ! plus rien contre la liberté ! plus rien par la force, par la violence, — si ce n'est contre la violence et la force, cela va sans dire.

L'ordre démocratique qui est l'ordre des choses modernes, ne connaitra qu'une puissance, la puissance de la liberté, l'ATTRAIT. Il doit abolir sur la terre toute loi de CONTRAINTE. Aussi, plus les peuples se démocratisent, plus toute contrainte leur devient odieuse.

Au moyen âge les peuples trouvaient tout simple qu'on les prît, qu'on les attachât ici ou là, qu'on les portât en dot de famille en famille, de couronne en couronne. Ils entraient dans les héritages, dans les marchés, dans les règlements d'affaires ou de guerre de Nos Seigneurs les conquérants féodaux. Ils étaient monnaie de princes, voilà tout, et passifs comme monnaie courante.

Aujourd'hui, ce n'est plus cela. Ils entendent être à eux-mêmes, s'appartenir exclusivement ; ils n'entendent plus obéir à personne ; ils veulent être leurs propres rois, leurs propres souverains, et ne relever d'autrui, qu'autrui soit un prince de droit divin ou un peuple étranger. Tous les peuples sont égaux, petits et grands, devant le droit moderne.

C'est pourquoi le peuple français, tout grand peuple initiateur qu'il soit en Europe, s'il ne se montrait entièrement, radicalement, absolument détaché de l'esprit du passé, dégagé de tout conquérantisme, de toute ambition territoriale, de toute pensée de contrainte ou de pression sur les peuples voisins, échouerait encore une fois dans son œuvre libératrice. C'est par la liberté, par la liberté seule qu'il doit faire les affaires de la liberté dans le monde. La liberté des peuples, c'est la liberté de Dieu, et tout attentat contre elle est un péché mortel.

L'Allemagne se tournait vers la France. Les vieilles haines étaient éteintes. Les deux grands peuples s'ouvraient l'un à l'autre et préludaient par leur rapprochement sympathique à la constitution du centre fédératif européen FRANCE-ALLEMAGNE. Arrive au pouvoir, le 1er mars 1840, M. Thiers. Le *Consulat* et l'*Empire* étaient dans son écritoire ; il en sortait des vapeurs de victoires et conquêtes. Ces vapeurs lui avaient monté au cerveau. Les Alpes et le Rhin lui faisaient tourner la tête. Dûment mystifié en Syrie par son magnanime ami et allié lord Palmerston, qu'il avait voulu y mystifier lui-même, il embouche la trompette, ordonne une levée de neuf cent mille hommes, fait sonner la charge par M. Léon Faucher et quelques autres chevaliers sans peur du journalisme. Louis-Philippe laisse faire, chante même la *Marseillaise*, tire ses fortifications de Paris du jeu, après quoi il chasse du ministère le petit vainqueur du Rhin (1).

_____

(1) Il paraît que M. Thiers, bien que devenu, dit-on, marguillier de Notre-Dame-de-Lorette, sa paroisse, n'en nourrit pas moins ses idées conquérantes. Le *Courrier français*, journal rédigé sous son influence, contenait dernièrement une agression des plus décidées contre la Belgique. On y lisait entre autres choses :

« La Belgique, telle que l'a créée la révolution de
» 1830, est devenue une tentation, une provocation
» continuelle qui peut troubler la paix de l'Europe.
» La Hollande la conquerrait en une quinzaine de
» jours, la Prusse en huit jours, et la France en 24
» heures. *Elle est aussi tentante et aussi résistante*
» *qu'un* PLUM-POUDING...
» *Nation sans nationalité, royaume sans autorité*
» *royale, république sans peuple,* elle est incapable
» de marcher autrement que comme ces impotents
» qui se roulent dans un fauteuil mécanique.

Hé bien ! il a suffi de ce ridicule accès de chauvinisme, de ce misérable tapage qui n'avait nul écho sérieux dans le pays, pour nous aliéner pendant plusieurs années l'Allemagne toute entière et changer, à nos portes, 40 millions d'amis en 40 millions d'ennemis. Est-ce vrai ?

A une autre époque, l'ancien *National*, qui était aussi un conquérant du Rhin, définissait dérisoirement la Belgique un *grand royaume situé dans les environs de Lille*, et parlait de n'en faire qu'une bouchée à la première occasion. J'étais en Belgique au moment où le *National* d'alors lançait ces sots articles. Je me rappelle l'effet. C'étaient quatre millions d'ennemis que le *National* donnait à la France en Belgique. Belle politique et joli cadeau !

Plus récemment, la stupide et odieuse affaire de *Risquons-Tout* ne fut-elle pas ce que l'on pouvait imaginer de mieux pour jeter la Belgique à la réaction européenne, et pour l'y maintenir, si cette échauffourée eût été un acte de gouvernement et non une aventure de cerveaux brûlés.

Et l'affaire de Chambéri ? On sait comment la population de cette ville, qui est pourtant française de langue, de mœurs, d'intérêts et de tendances, a reçu l'expédition armée qui prétendait la révolutionner pour le compte de la République française.

Non ! en permanence et en principe, la démocratie française déclare la guerre à la maison d'Autriche, parce que cette maison est en flagrant et permanent délit d'oppression sur l'Italie, la Hongrie et autres peuples.

Elle déclare la guerre, pour cause analogue, au czar, égorgeur de la Pologne. Voilà les ennemis, et, en supposant qu'elle ne soit pas attaquée la première, les cas d'initiative de guerre de la Démocratie française en Europe.

Dans les mêmes intérêts, pour le même but

_____

» Jamais la Belgique n'a su ce qu'était l'indépen
» dance... Elle est dans une crise de *catalepsie*. Elle
» a tout juste assez de sens pour savoir que, si on la
» remue un doigt, il y a tout près d'elle trois
» grands chirurgiens prêts à *la saigner*... »

Voilà comment les gens de l'école de M. Thiers entendent les droits des faibles. Vous vous sentez et vous vous affirmez nationalité, on vous répond : Non, vous n'êtes pas une nationalité, et la preuve, c'est que vous avez des voisins qui peuvent vous avaler d'une bouchée.

Que de telles doctrines apprennent du moins aux faibles qu'il n'y a de refuge et de véritable sécurité pour eux que dans les principes et la victoire du droit démocratique, dans le triomphe de l'école de la fraternité.

L'Empire en France, ce serait, de façon ou d'autre, l'ambition du Rhin et des Alpes, l'absorption de la Belgique et toutes les mauvaises traditions de *mon oncle*. On y marcherait par des coups de tête ou par de tortueuses combinaisons diplomatiques.

et le même principe, la Démocratie française proclame respect et au besoin défend l'indépendance des faibles et l'inviolabilité des neutres.

La Suisse et la Belgique veulent être neutres. C'est leur intérêt, leur droit et, de plus, leur devoir et leur mission.

La Suisse peut mettre 80,000 hommes sous les armes, défendre ou livrer son sol et ses passages.

La Belgique peut également mettre 80,000 hommes sous les armes, défendre ou livrer son sol et ses places fortes.

Ces deux Etats sont les deux boulevards de la France.

Si la France, à un moment quelconque, sous un prétexte quelconque, fut-ce celui de sûreté, commettait la faute et le *crime de menacer la neutralité de l'un ou de l'autre de ces Etats, à l'instant cet Etat serait un boulevard ouvert à nos ennemis, une citadelle faisant, sur un front de 80 lieues, feu contre nous.

Qu'au contraire, fidèle au principe capital de la démocratie socialiste, la France proclame le droit souverain de ces Etats à la liberté, à l'indépendance nationale, et se porte forte pour leur inviolabilité, l'ennemi ne pouvant tenter rien de sérieux contre nous qu'en attentant à cette inviolabilité, dès que les armées de la coalition font mine de marcher sur les Alpes ou sur la Meuse, ces Etats attaqués tiennent pour nous et nous appellent.

CONCLUSION.

Egalité, Liberté, Fraternité !

Egalité des forts et des faibles devant la loi moderne, Liberté et Fraternité des Peuples : voilà l'esprit de la Démocratie sociale, sa formule, sa politique et son irrésistible puissance.

Nous sommes le parti de l'Ordre européen ! Nous sommes plus qu'un parti, nous sommes une Religion, le vrai Christianisme des individus, des peuples et des races, le vrai Catholicisme, le Catholicisme démocratique et social.

Satan, c'est *la guerre*. l'oppression, l'exploitation, la violence et la contrainte sous toutes leurs formes.

Dieu, c'est l'Amour et la Liberté. Sa loi, c'est l'Attrait. Son Verbe, c'est la voix des peuples qui veulent être libres et s'unir. Les temps sont venus, *Vade retro Satanas* !

Mazzini, Kossuth, Ledru-Rollin, et vous, chefs de la démocratie allemande, et vous tous, qui, de Cadix à Varsovie, évangélisez la Religion de l'Humanité, conspirons ensemble, conspirons éloignés et dispersés; conspirons en plein soleil ! Les paroles des martyrs de la liberté, des proscrits de tous les pays, sont des paroles sacrées. Victimes expiatoires des fautes commises, des malentendus des peuples, de la violence de leurs oppresseurs, conspirons la paix du monde, l'indépendance et la fraternité des peuples ! Que les peuples, longtemps désunis et hostilisés par l'ancien esprit barbare, par le machiavélisme des deux maisons impériales du Nord, et par les derniers échos de l'impérialisme français, se donnent réciproquement des gages par la voix de tous ceux qui parlent pour eux ! Que chacun traduise dans sa langue les formules saintes de la démocratie sociale, dissipe les craintes réciproques, fasse briller la pensée de paix, de liberté pour tous, de solidarité européenne ! Disposons les cœurs à la pratique du christianisme social. Confédération des peuples libres, fondation de l'ordre européen, paix perpétuelle, telle est l'Idéal de la démocratie moderne. Faisons éclater partout la révélation de cet Idéal, et l'Idéal d'aujourd'hui sera demain la Réalité.

Voilà notre conspiration. Les despotes se préparent à faire tonner le canon, c'est leur métier. Faisons tonner la fraternité, c'est le nôtre. Aux armes donc ! aux armes ! pour la dernière guerre. Nos armes sont, avant tout, nos principes, nos sentiments et nos idées. TOUS LES PEUPLES SONT FRÈRES. *Hoc verbo vinces.*

20 mars 1850.

EXTRAIT DU CATALOGUE

DE LA LIBRAIRIE PHALANSTÉRIENNE, RUE DE BEAUNE, 2, ET QUAI VOLTAIRE, 25.

OUVRAGES DE FOURIER :

THÉORIE DE L'UNITÉ UNIVERSELLE. C'est l'ouvrage capital de Fourier. (2ᵉ édition, 4 forts volumes in-8°, contenant le *Plan du Traité de l'Attraction.* et quatre vignettes. (Tomes II, III, IV et V des œuvres complètes), 18 fr. — Chaque volume séparément, 4 fr. 50.

LE NOUVEAU MONDE INDUSTRIEL ET SOCIÉTAIRE. Abrégé du précédent, (mais néanmoins difficile à lire sans préparation.) 5ᵉ édition, 1 fort vol. in-8°. (Tome IV des œuvres complètes.) 5 fr.

THÉORIE DES 4 MOUVEMENTS. (Ne peut être lu avec fruit que comme complément d'études, après une connaissance avancée de la Théorie.) 5ᵉ édit., 1 fort vol. in 8°, (Tome I des œuvres complètes.) 6 fr.
Les 6 volumes précédents ensemble 28 francs.

L'HARMONIE UNIVERSELLE ET LE PHALANSTÈRE, exposés par Charl s FOURIER, recueil méthodique de morceaux choisis de l'auteur.—Prix : 6 fr. 2 vol. format Charpentier, 3 fr. le vol.

DE L'ANARCHIE INDUSTRIELLE ET SCIENTIFIQUE. — Brochure in-12 de 72 pages.—Prix : 75 c.; par la poste, 1 fr.

LIVRET D'ANNONCE du NOUVEAU MONDE INDUSTRIEL. Broch. de 88 pages in-8°.—Prix : 1 fr.; par la poste, 1 fr. 40 c.

ÉGAREMENT DE LA RAISON démontré par les ridicules des sciences incertaines, et *fragments.*—Brochure de 128 pages grand in-8°—Prix : 2 fr. 50 c.; par la poste, 2 fr. 80 c.

ANALYSE DU MÉCANISME DE L'AGIOTAGE et de la méthode mixte en étude de l'attraction.—Brochure de 128 pages grand in-8°.—Prix : 2 fr.; par la poste, 2 fr. 50 c.

SUR L'ESPRIT IRRÉLIGIEUX DES MODERNES ET DERNIÈRES ANALOGIES, par Charles FOURIER. (Extrait de la *Phalange.*) Prix : 1 fr.; par la poste, 1 f. 10.

CITÉS OUVRIÈRES. DES MODIFICATIONS A INTRODUIRE DANS L'ARCHITECTURE DES VILLES.—Brochure de 40 pages grand in-8.—Prix : 50 c.; par la poste, 40 c.

OUVRAGES DES PRINCIPAUX DISCIPLES DE FOURIER :

DESTINÉE SOCIALE, Exposition élémentaire complète de la THÉORIE D'ORGANISATION SOCIALE DE FOURIER, par Victor CONSIDÉRANT. — Prix : 5 fr.—3ᵉ édition, 2 volumes format Charpentier.—Chaque vol., 2 fr. 50 c.

LE SOCIALISME DEVANT LE VIEUX MONDE, par V. Considérant. 1 vol. in-8. Prix : 2 fr.; par la poste, 2 fr. 50.

PRINCIPES DU SOCIALISME, Manifeste de la Démocratie au XIXᵉ siècle, par Victor Considérant. In 18. Prix : 50 c.; par la poste, 75 c.

MANIFESTE DE **L'ÉCOLE SOCIÉTAIRE** fondée par FOURIER, ou BASES DE LA POLITIQUE POSITIVE. Paris, 1842, (écrit par M. CONSIDÉRANT, et adopté par le Conseil de l'École). Nouvelle édition, revue et considérablement augmentée. 1847. Un beau vol, in-18. Prix : 1 fr.; par la poste, 1 fr. 35 c.

EXPOSITION abrégée du système phalanstérien, suivi des études sur quelques problèmes fondamentaux de la destinée sociale, par Victor Considérant, grand in-32. Prix : 50 c.; par la poste, 75 c.
— *Le même ouvrage* sans les études. Prix : 25 c.; par la poste, 35 c.

DU SENS VRAI DE LA RÉDEMPTION, par Victor CONSIDÉRANT, *morceau détaché de la troisième edition de* DESTINÉE SOCIALE.—Prix : 1 fr.

PETIT COURS de politique et d'économie sociale à l'usage des ignorants et des savants, par Victor Considérant. In-18. Prix : 40 c.; par la poste, 50 c.

DÉBÂCLE de la politique en France, par V. Considérant. In-18. Prix : 1 fr.; par la poste, 1 fr. 25 c.

PAROLE DE **PROVIDENCE** par Mᵐᵉ CLARISSE VIGOUREUX, 2ᵉ éd. Prix : 1 f.; par la poste, 1 fr. 25 c.

LE FOU DU PALAIS-ROYAL, par F. CANTAGREL. Dialogues sur la théorie de Fourier. 2ᵉ édition. 1 fort vol. grand in-18, format Charpentier. Prix : 5 fr.; par la poste, 4 fr.

SOLIDARITÉ, vue synthétique sur la doctrine de FOURIER, par Hipp. RENAUD, ancien élève de l'École polytechnique.—1 vol. in-18. Prix : 1 fr. 25 c.; par la poste, 1 fr. 50 c.

L'ORGANISATION DU TRAVAIL ET L'ASSOCIATION, par Mathieu BRIANCOURT, ouvrier teinturier.—2ᵉ édition. Un vol. in-32. Prix : 60 c.; par la poste, 80 c.

VISITE AU PHALANSTÈRE, par Mathieu Briancourt. In-32. Prix : 1 fr. 50 c.; par la poste, 1 fr. 80 c.

FOURIER, SA VIE ET SA THÉORIE, par Charles PELLARIN. — Troisième édition entièrement revue par l'auteur, et contenant, entres autres documents inédits, une lettre de M. ENFANTIN à FOURIER, et une lettre de Béranger sur Fourier et sa Théorie.—1 gros volume in-18.—Prix : 5 fr.; et par la poste 4 fr.